PHILOSOPHY OF HISTORY

Some Reflections on North-East India

Dr. S.C. Daniel

Regency Publications
New Delhi 110 008

Division of
DAYA PUBLISHING HOUSE
4760-61/23, Ansari Road,
Darya Ganj, New Delhi - 110 002
Phone: 23245578, 23244987; Fax: (011) 23260116
E-mail: info@regency-books.com
Website: www.regencybooks.com

ISBN 81-87498-08-0

Published by Regency Publications, 20/36-G, Old Market, West Patel Nagar, New Delhi 110 008 and Printed at Radiant Printers, New Delhi 110 008, Phones: 574 0038, 571 2539; Telefax: 578 3571

www.regencypublications.com
Email: *regency@satyam.net.in* and *info@regencypublications.com*

Foreword

While history is basically a science for the study of development in a period or over some periods of time, the philosophy of history essentially aims at determining the nature and significance of that development in a logical way. In other words, both are interested in human past, though the historian's concern is the understanding and analysis of the past, while the philosopher of history would draw on historical writings for a comprehensive explanation of the historical processes and conceptualization of these processes. The fact that history by nature is more analytic and more explanatory than chronicle of account or narrative of the past is justifying enough to explain its causal dependence. And for the same reason, the historians are also philosophers in their own field. They not only describe a development but also explain the causes and effects of such a development. They make the facts speak for themselves in complete nuances and ramifications and go further to explain if something had happened, why did it happen, and if not, why not. The basic tools of a historian are the data or source material, but he also reads between the lines and applies his mind to link the text and the context, to interpret the information and to draw the conclusions and formulations. These conclusions and formulations draw him closer to the philosophers of history who use the historical writings to conceptualize the human past and to predict the future on the basis of historical explanations. To a philosopher of history, the causal explanation relates to the past and teleological explanation points to the future; and to a historian, the future is predicted on the basis of the past. The past is an experience and an index to what may come in the future. The lesson of history is that if the conditions which contributed to a particular situation or event or development in the past do repeat then one should be ready to face same situation or event or development under similar conditions.

The processes in the history of mankind are older than the discipline called history and these processes came into action as soon as the man dawned on earth. The civilizations in different parts of our planet experienced these processes, or at least some of these, at different points of time and this fact explains why the levels of development differ from region to region. The conditions which determine the courses of history appeared in some region later, or even much later, than others. The North-Eastern Region of India, or North East India, which stands between two important geographical divisions representing two great civilizations of the world, namely, Indian and Chinese, is known for geographical, ethnic, linguistic, cultural and economic diversities in itself. Described by Dr. Suniti Kumar Chattopadhyay as "the Eastern Gateway for passage of Peoples, Commodities and Ideas between China and India", the total geographical area of the region today is 2,55,037 square kilometres. Its international boundary with Bangladesh, Myanmar (Burma), China (including Tibet) and Bhutan runs to 4,200 kilometres, while it is connected with the rest of India by the narrow 'Siliguri neck' of less than 20 kilometres in North Bengal. The major portion of the region is hilly. Arunachal Pradesh, Meghalaya, Mizoram and Nagaland are hill states with minor patches or dots of dales and valleys, while Assam, Manipur and Tripura cover both hills and plains. The Brahmaputra and the Barak, both of which ultimately confluence in the Meghna in East Bengal (now Bangladesh) are the two great rivers of the region. The Brahmaputra Valley and the Barak Valley (the latter includes the adjoining plains portion of Tripura) are the major plains tracts connected with Northern Bengal and the South-East Bengal respectively. The Manipur Valley is virtually encircled by the hills, barring a narrow plains tract provided by the slim trans-Barak basin which connects the Manipur Valley with the Barak Valley. The

Brahmaputra Valley, which is the largest plains tract in the region, extends for about 600 kilometres from Sadiya in the East to Dhubri in West Assam where the Brahmaputra turns towards the south and along the western edge of the Garo Hills of Meghalaya. The valley of the Brahmaputra is only about 75 kilometres wide and it was easily accessible from Bengal plains on the west even in early times. Barring the opening to Bengal plains near Dhubri that forms a narrow neck, the rest of the Valley is bordered by a continuous hills chain in succession, by the Meghalaya plateau or Assam range, Naga hills, Arunachal hills and Bhutan, like a garland. The valleys of Brahmaputra and the Barak are separated from each other by a segment of the Assam range, i.e. North Cachar Hills, immediately intervening between the two. The Barak Valley-Tripura plains tract, which is commonly called Ishan Banga or North-East Bengal, is bounded on three sides by the North Cachar hills, Manipur hills, Mizo hills and the Chittagong hills forming virtually a high wall, while on the fourth it is followed in slow succession by the plains districts of Bengal without disturbing the landscape. The hills division starts from the western slope of the Garo hills. Khasi-Jaintia hills, and the North Cachar hills, and then it joins the Mikir (Karbi) hills, Naga hills, Arunachal hills and the Bhutan hills, which together form part of the Eastern Himalayas. The Naga hills, Manipur hills, Mizo hills and the adjoining hills in Burma also form a chain of mountain ranges. The Brahmaputra Valley, Meghalaya hills, Barak Valley and Tripura thus directly border Bengal, while Manipur and Tripura has direct access to Burma, Arunachal to Tibet (China) and Assam to Bhutan. No wonder, despite the geographical and political isolation and difficult terrains, the states and tribal formations in North East India maintained commercial contacts between the natural divisions and also across these divisions, through buffer zones and communities, in the region as well as with neighbouring Bengal, Bhutan, Tibet, China and Burma since time immemorial.

The migrations and settlement of the peoples in the region in earliest periods of historical development also occurred on the basis of direct accessibility. The migrations were through the easily available routes. The Indo-Aryans and the

Tibeto-Burmans migrated from the respective directions and settled down in the easily accessible divisions and settled down permanently. In the earliest stage of development the Tibeto-Burmans or the Austrics and Mongolians of Tiber, China, Burma, Thailand and Laos migrated and settled all over the region. The Indo-Aryans then migrated and settled in the valleys of Brahmaputra and the Barak. These two divisions were since then integrated in the pan-Indian cultural continuum and there was a spontaneous assimilation of the Indo-Aryan and the Indo-Mogoloids in these divisions. The earliest state formations of Brahmanical Hindu model were also noticed in these two divisions at least since the fifth century AD. The Pragjyotisha-Kamarupa and the Harikela were the earliest known states in the valleys of Brahmaputra and the Barak respectively. The Barak Valley sector was included in the Samata State of Eastern and South-Eastern Bengal for most of the early periods. In seventh century for a short period a portion of the Barak valley formed part of Kamarupa under Bhaskar Varman. Thereafter, there was the revival of Samata and Harikela in quick successions. In 10th century, the Barak Valley was included in the Vanga State of East Bengal. After the decline of Vanga, Shrihatta Rajya emerged as an autonomous state in this Valley. In the Brahmaputra Valley, the decline of Kamarupa was followed by emergence of a number of smaller states ruled by local dynasties. One of these, the Salasthambha dynasty was possibly of a Bodo tribal origin. This indicates the type of cultural assimilation that was in operation at least in the plains tracts of the region. The history of these dynasties is known from the inscriptions, coins, archaeological remains and literary sources. Sanskrit language was used by the local rulers for official purposes. Some of the rivers and hills of the region were mentioned in the ancient Indian literature as holy. The Parasurama Kundyo in Arunachal Pradesh, Kamakshya in Assam, Siddheswara in Barak Valley, Unakuti in Tripura etc were respected as holy shrines all over India. In the medieval period, the state formation processes of the same model extended beyond the two valleys. The Ahom, Koch, Dimasa Kachari, Jaintia, Tripuri, Manipuri (Meitei) were among the important medieval states of the region. Assamese and Bengali languages developed during this period, and these two languages, besides Sanskrit, Ahom and Meitei, were used in local courts. The medieval period is also known for several invasions from Bengal. Though most of these invasions were unsuccessful, the parts of Lower Assam and Barak Valley passed under Mughal rule and some of the local rulers temporarily acknowledged Mughal suzerainty. Nevertheless, the Mughal contacts positively influenced the social, economic and cultural life of the region. The Bhakti-Sufi movements made deep impacts in Assam and Barak Valley as in case of rest of India. The famous saint, Sankạradeva of Assam was a great social reformer and he contributed greatly to the development of modern Assamese language and literature. The Vaisnava movement of Shri Chaitanya in Bengal became a strong movement in Barak Valley and there from, it penetrated into Manipur. The settled cultivation, terrace and plough started in the plains in early times, whereas in the hills, jhumming and tribal social and political formations continued throughout the ancient and medieval periods. Nevertheless, the economic relations between the hills and the plains were maintained through the markets which emerged in the foothills. The barter was the dominant mode of economy. The surplus produces of the villages were exchanged with the neighbours to balance the deficits. The markets also played a very important role in exchange of ideas and cultural contacts between the hills and the plains and the various communities in the region. In the nineteenth century, the British occupied the region in several instalments and integrated it in their Indian colonial state. The Christian Missions came in the British period and since then the Christianity made a strong impact, particularly in the hills. The western education and English language were also introduced in the same period. The tribal languages were reduced to writing in Roman script at the initiative of missionaries. In most of these languages, today we have rich literature. The British rule also saw the opening up of the region through roads and railways and other means of communication. The exploitation of oil and coal deposits started and the tea industry was introduced. Some other minor industries also made a beginning, though the traditional art and crafts received a set back and the rural economy lost its autonomy. Modern education, administration and urbanisation became major factors of social change to which the people of the region spontaneously responded. Before long, craze for white collar job became the order. A dominant middle class came in the scene. The region positively responded to India's national struggle for freedom. After independence, Assam has been reorganised in phases into four states. NEFA has been separated from Assam and gradually elevated to the status of a State. Manipur and Tripura, which were princely states in the British period, are also fulfledged states. The North-Eastern Council and a common High Court with Benches in the state capitals are the unifying factors today, though the geographical contiguity, historical linkages, economic backwardness and a general feeling of isolation and indifference of the central authority are more dominant unifying forces.

North East India passed through the historical processes which were experienced in rest of India and the neighbouring countries, particularly South and South-East Asia. The factors and stages of historical development of human society like hunting and gathering, neolithic revolution and the dawn of the metal age; domestication of animals, beginning of agriculture and the village formations; evolution of customs and practices, traditional institutions and institutional change; social stratification, communal holdings; transition from tribal to complex societies; agriculture, crafts and industry; emergence of private property; State formations; barter to money economy; short and long distance trade; co-existence of tribal and non-tribal societies; religion, value system and new values; illiteracy, literacy and education for some; tribal polity, monarchy, feudal order; rise and fall of states and kingdoms; imperialism and colonialism; urbanisation; emergence and hegemony of the middle class; social reforms, philanthropists and philosophers; modern democracy, local self-government; ethnic conflicts, communal and linguistic violence, peasants and workers movements, class struggle; nationalism; extremist and secessionist movements; etc. have all been experienced in this region. Therefore, the global perceptions of the philosophers of history and the historical explanations offered in specific contexts and in similar conditions are likely to be relevant to the region.

Dr. S.C. Daniel's *Philosophy of History: Some Reflections on North East-India* is the first and a serious attempt at an understanding of the subject. The book is a collection of eight papers presented by the author in the annual sessions of the North East India History Association (NEIHA) between 1991 and 1998. He discussed the views of eight globally acclaimed philosophers, viz. David Hume, Immanuel Kant, George William Friedrich Hegel, Karl Marx, Shri Aurobindo and Karl Raimand Popper. To apply the theories of these great thinkers, Dr. Daniel drew mainly on the writings of six historians of North East India, viz. S.K. Bhuyan, H.K. Barpujari, Amalendu Guha, N.N. Bhattacharjee, J.B. Bhattacharjee and D.R. Syiemlieh. In first two chapters of the book, he discussed the logic of historical analysis in the context of North East Indian historiography and the objectivity and history as a case study of North East India. Between these two chapters, Dr. Daniel has broadly reviewed the formulations of the great philosophers of history of the world vis-à-vis the historiography of North east India on a selective basis and stated his own positioning of the better known historians of the region. Equally interesting is his introduction wherein he states his own arguments about the merit of historical explanations. In the chapter on objectivity, he discusses and rejects at least eight criterions of achieving objectivity as formulated by well known scholars, and adds a ninth, called 'relative objectivity', which, according to him, "is sustained and preserved by the continuity of historical inquiry without ignoring the significance of historical facts". He further states that "the task of historiographer is to maintain and preserve the continuity of historical inquiry so as to have a holistic account of such an inquiry". He is "convinced that history is capable of achieving this purpose by adopting the ninth criterion." This position of the author may generate a debate in philosophy of history and several eye-brows are likely to be raised on his positioning of the historians of North East India. Nevertheless, it is a well known fact that research flourishes through debates and controversies and the scholars contribute more positively by agreeing to disagree. I wish that this call is responded to by the scholars in spirit it has been forwarded. Dr. Daniel will also certainly welcome a scholarly debate on the subject and his efforts will be rewarded only when this debate leads to a better understanding of the historiography of North East India.

I have known Dr. S.C. Daniel as an esteemed colleague at NEHU for more than two decades and I have always appreciated his scholarly devotion to his work and interdisciplinary interests. We enjoyed discussing some of the issues which are common between history and philosophy and mutually learnt from each other both by agreeing and disagreeing. The papers presented by him in NEIHA sessions always evinced keen interests and provoked serious discussions. I congratulate him for the decision to bring out those papers in a single collection.

Silchar
15 April 1999

(J.B. BHATTACHARJEE)
Vice-Chancellor
Assam University
Silchar 788 011

Acknowledgements

I wish to express my thanks to Professor J.B. Bhattacharjee, Vice-Chancellor of Assam University, Silchar, for his generous foreword to this book. I feel that I do not deserve the compliments which Professor J.B. Bhattacharjee has very magnanimously showered on me. I must thank Dr. C. Joshua Thomas, Deputy Director, North-Eastern Regional Centre of the Indian Council of Social Science Research, Shillong, for his valuable encouragement and timely help. It is no exaggeration to say that without his valuable support this book would not have seen the light of the day. I owe my gratitude to Professors J.B. Bhattacharjee, Milton S. Sangma, Imdad Hussain, and J.P. Singh, and Drs. D.R. Syiemlieh and Manorama Sharma of the Department of History of North-Eastern Hill University for making me a member of North-East India History Association (NEIHA), and for encouraging me to present papers on Philosophy of History in the annual sessions of this renowned organisation. I gratefully acknowledge my debt to the North East India History Association (NEIHA) for giving me the opportunity to present my papers in its Annual Sessions held at Jagi Road, Assam; North-Eastern Hill University, Shillong, Meghalaya; Jorhat, Assam; Doimukh, Arunachal University, Arunachal Pradesh; Silchar, Assam University, Silchar, Assam; Aizawl, the capital of Mizoram; Agartala, Tripura University, Tripura; and Kohima, the capital of Nagaland; and also for publishing seven of the papers in the Twelfth (1991), Thirteenth (1993), Fourteenth (1993), Fifteenth (1994), Sixteenth (1995), Seventeenth (1996) and Eithteenth (1997) Proceedings volumes. The eighth paper was read at the Nineteenth Session (1998). I thank the North-East India History Association for the permission to publish these articles in this collection. I take this opportunity to thank Shri Joseph F. Khongbuh, for typing the manuscript with utmost love, care and efficiency. Thanks for my wife, Mrs. Diana Daniel, and for my sons, Collins Tilak Daniel and Robert Chandran Daniel for sharing my struggle and anxiety with enduring love and affection. I must thank my University, North-Eastern Hill University, Shillong, for supporting me with financial assistance to attend the annual sessions of NEIHA held in various places of North-East India.

S.C. Daniel

Contents

Papers Presented at Annual Sessions of the North East India History Association

1. "The Logic of Historical Analysis: Reflection on North-Eastern Historiography," Twelfth Session, Jagi Road, 1991.
2. "Objectivity and History: A Case Study of North East India", Thirteenth Session, Shillong, 1993.
3. "Karl Popper and the Poverty of Historicism – A Critical Approach", Fourteenth Session, Jorhat, 1993.
4. "Hegel's Philosophy of History: A Critical Evaluation", Fifteenth Session, 1994.
5. "Hume's Theory of History: A Conspectus", Sixteenth Session, Assam University, Silchar, 1995.
6. "Karl Marx's Theory of History", Seventeenth Session, Government Aizawl College, Aizawl, 1996.
7. "Sri Aurobindo's Theory of History: A Philosophical Investigation", Eighteenth Session, Tripura University, Agartala, 1997.
8. "Kant's Philosopphy of History: A Conspectus", Nineteenth Session, Nagaland University, Kohima, 1998.

CHAPTER 1

Introduction

The function of philosophy of history was considered to be one that of determining the nature and significance of the human past. And this concept of history of philosophy was held to be valid and correct until almost the end of nineteenth century. Philosophy of history so regarded has had a long and distinguished career beginning from Graeco-Roman times and ending with the grand theories expounded by great philosophers of history such as Vico, Hegel, Comte, and Marx. This traditional view of philosophy of history claimed that the philosophers of history were primarily concerned with the same subject-matter as historians in the over simplified way as mentioned earlier, however, approaching it from a different direction, which was at variance with that of the historians. The philosophers of history were occupied with the ambitious programme of offering an all-comprehensive interpretation of the historical process as a *whole*, and not with the rather limited and partial inquiries that were to be found in ordinary historical work. In other words, the philosophers of history aimed at a *holistic* approach. However, it must be pointed out that these philosophers of history more often than not conceptualized the past in different ways. Of these different ways, two are very fundamental and important, which are as follows: (1) Perceiving the past as manifesting a *unilinear progression* towards a better state, and (2) perceiving a cyclical pattern of the past that involved the continuous repetition of recognizable models of growth and decay. Those philosophers of history who belong to category (2) differ from each other as regards the principles that govern those continual recurrence of identifiable patterns of growth and decay. Some considered those patterns as governed by causal or mechanistic principles akin to those explained by physical sciences while some depended on rational or teleological concepts which helped them to find in history a manifestation of certain logical principles or *unitary design*. Some believed in necessary or deterministic order to which the sequence of events conformed while some other found room for some sort of contingency or freedom. But, whatever differences of perspectives and importance there may have been, they were all concerned with a *substantive* or *factual branch of study* that dealt directly with the phenomenon of human affairs albeit from a lofty point of view.

The present century, that is, the twentieth century, has been witnessing a radical change in the conception of philosophy of history. The central aspiration of the classical conception of philosophy of history to offer a total explanatory account of the past is not being regarded sympathetically in the present century. The classical philosophers are being criticized for working with an imprecise and vague conceptual apparatus. They are also being criticized of formulating hypotheses which are considered to be rather unclear and arbitrary. The general complaint against the classical or traditional conception of philosophy of history is that it depended on unexamined *a priori* assumptions. The methodology of the classical philosophy of history is found to be inadequate since it is scientifically oriented. At present times, philosophy of history is regarded as a second-order inquiry or criteriology. And this second-order inquiry or criteriology tries to explain and judge the ways in which historians describe or understand the past. The philosophy of history of *Analytic Age* analyses the presuppositions of historical narratives, the various categories of historical judgement and explanation, and the arguments to support or establish the conclusions arrived at. Needless to point out that it has become essentially analytical and conceptual.

It may not be out of place here to make a distinction between history and philosophy of history. Needless to point out that a discussion on the nature of philosophy of history is a precondition for writing a book on philosophy of history. Philosophers and historians differ in their views as to the nature of this branch of philosophy. Even the practising philosophers of history agree to disagree with each other about the proper subject matter of this unique discipline. To determine the nature as well as the exact subject matter of this discipline, it will be helpful to discuss four familiar and yet important viewpoints on this matter albeit in a rather perfunctory manner. According to the first view, it is the business of the philosophers of history to emphasize the broader and metaphysical implications of philosophy of history, which consists in speculating about the ontological categories that are to be used in talking about 'being-as-such'. The second view assigns the task of giving an exposition of the pre-suppositions and pre-dispositions of the historians to the philosopher of history. Adopting this view, the philosopher of history may point out that the historians pre-suppose that there is some sort of order in nature, and he may point that the preferences of the historians for deterministic laws, or for mechanistic rather than teleological explanation. The third view treats philosophy of history as a discipline which analyses and clarifies the concepts and theories of history. This is to say that there are certain types of conceptual analysis that should be classified as part of philosophy of history. What types of conceptual analysis are they? The fourth view of philosophy of history answers this crucial question. This view is that philosophy of history is a second-order criteriology, which seeks to answer the following kinds of questions: (i) What are the distinguishing features of historical inquiry? (ii) What procedures should be prescribed to historians in investigating the human past? (iii) What conditions must a historical explanation satisfy in order to be correct? This view recognizes three orders of discipline, namely, 0 (zero) level order, first level order, and second level order. The following chart brings out the distinction between these three levels crystal clear.

Level	Discipline	Subject matter
0	None	Facts
1	History	Explanation of the human past.
2	Philosophy of History	Analysis of the Procedures and Logic of Historical Explanations.

It may be noted here that it is not possible to draw an absolute and sharp distinctions between history and philosophy of history; for the distinction can be based only on a difference of *intent* rather than a difference of subject matter.

The title of my book is, *Philosophy of History: Some Reflections on North-East India.* I must confess that I have been able to discuss the views of very few philosophers of history such as David Hume, Kant, Hegel, Marx, Karl Popper, and Sri Aurobindo. This is not to say that there are no other equally important philosophers of history; in fact, there are. I have not also been able to include all the historians of North-East India. However, the historians of North-East India that I have included such as S.K. Bhuyan, J.B: Bhattacharjee, H.K. Barpujari, A. Guha, N.N. Bhattacharyya, and D.R. Syiemlieh are fair and true representatives of this region; for they are some of the most important and eminent historians of this beautiful region of our country.

The book consists of eight chapters. The first chapter is entitled *"The Logic of Historical Analysis: Reflections on North-Eastern Historiography"*. This chapter tries to establish that history is not a purely ideographic science, and that there is no fundamental difference between the logical structure of explanation in historical and generalizing science. A few instances from the historical writings on North-East India have been cited to substantiate this thesis.

The second chapter is on *"Objectivity and History: A Case Study of North East India"*. The chapter considers eight criteria of objectivity in a nutshell and rejects them as being vacuous or empty or unintelligent or expressionless. A ninth criterion is proposed to indicate that history has 'relative' objectivity. Instances from writings on North-East India have been used to bring out the relevance of the proposed criterion.

The third chapter gives a conspectus of *Hume's Theory of History*. Hume's addition theory of knowledge is highlighted here. It has been pointed out that though Hume is a particularist in epistemology, metaphysics, and religion, he seems to uphold universalism in history. Hume's theory of history is made relevant in case of the historical writings on North-East India.

Kant's Philosophy of History forms the fourth chapter in which an attempt is made to reconstruct Kant's Philosophy of History logically with the help of his History of Reason, History as the Moral Totality and The History of Philosophy and its Architectonic. As it has been my wont, the writings on North-East India have been related to Kant's Philosophy of History.

The fifth chapter critically evaluates *Hegel's Philosophy of History*. The historical writings of the eminent historian S. K. Bhuyan on North East India have been cited as an example of his closeness to at least one of the fundamental principles of Hegel's philosophy of History.

The sixth chapter on *"Karl Marx's Theory of History"* tries to explicate Karl Marx's theory of history as a normative one. In this connection, a normative approach has been suggested to understand better the multi-ethnic, multi-cultural, multi-linguistic and multi-religious North-Eastern society.

The seventh chapter is concerned with one of the greatest philosophers of modern India. It discusses *Sri Aurobindo's Theory of History* with the help of Hegelian Idealism, Indian Idealism and Universalism, especially with regard to religion. It also connects Sri Aurobindo's theory with that of some historical writings on North-East India.

The eighth chapter deals with *"Karl Popper and the Poverty of Historicism"*. It tries to invalidate the argument of Popper, which tries to refute historicism. As in the other chapters, I have drawn some inspiration from the historical writings on North-East India in order to provide substance to my argument.

CHAPTER 2

The Logic of Historical Analysis: Reflections on North Eastern Historiography

It is widely held that there is a distinction between two types of science, namely, nomothetic and ideographic.[1] The nomothetic science seeks to establish abstract general laws for infinitely repeatable processes while the ideographic science aims to understand the unique and the non-recurrent. It is often maintained that natural sciences are nomothetic, and that history (in the sense of an account of events) is ideographic. It is also generally claimed that the logic and conceptual structure of historical explanations are fundamentally different from those of natural sciences. This chapter makes an attempt to show that history is not a purely ideographic science, and that there is no radical difference between the logical structure of explanation in historical and generalizing sciences. A few examples from the historical writings on North-East India have been discussed to strengthen this position.

There is, in fact, a *prima facie* difference between theoretical natural sciences and history, which is as follows. The statements of the former are usually general in form while almost all the statements of the latter are singular, which make use of proper names, dates, geographic specifications, language, literature, sociological factors, and so on. Thus, for example, Professor J.B. Bhattacharjee considers the historical developments in the Barak Valley essentially as an extension of Bengal phenomenon on the basis of geographical and sociological structure of that valley. He makes use of the names of places, rivers and hills to substantiate his contentions.[2] I am inclined to believe that he offers this explanation as a logical one. It would, however, be erroneous to conclude that singular statements have no place in the theoretical sciences, or that universal or general statements have no place in historical inquiry. I claim that historical inquiry makes use of general statements for the following reason. Historians often aim to be more than mere chroniclers of the past by attempting to understand and explain recorded action in terms of their causes and consequences. In order to do this, they must assume certain well-established laws of causal dependence. Nonetheless, there is an important asymmetry between theoretical and historical sciences, which consists in the fact that the former try to establish laws while the latter desist from doing so.

Do the logic and conceptual structure of historical explanation differ in *kind* from that of natural sciences? My answer is in the negative. And the argument, which establishes my negative answer, is as follows. It has been said that there is a *formal* difference between the 'general concepts' of the theoretical sciences and the 'individual concepts', which are assumed to be the goals of historical inquiry. The concepts of the former sort are allged to conform to the familiar logical principle of the inverse variation of the extension and intention of terms, that is, when a set of general terms is arranged in order of their increasing extensions, their intentions decrease while in the case of the concepts of the latter sort, quite the opposite is said to hold good, that is, greater the scope of such a concept, the richer and fuller would be its 'meaning'. For example, the term 'French Enlightenment' is claimed to have not only a more inclusive scope than the term 'the life of Voltaire' but also to possess a fuller intention. This is simply a confusion. And this confusion is not least due to the failure to distinguish the relation of *inclusion* from that of whole-part relation between an instance of a term and a component of that term. Thus, though the term 'French Enlightenment' may be said to 'contain' as one of its 'components', 'the life of Voltaire', it is a mistake to say that the *extension* of the former term includes the *extension* of the latter term.

What is historical analysis? Historical analysis consists in giving historical explanation. What is an explanation? The term 'explanation' is derived from two terms, namely, *ex* and *plano*, which means 'out of' and to 'make plain' respectively. The term, therefore, literally means *making plain or clear something which appears to be obscure or mysterious*. What is historical explanation? This vital question can be answered by making a sharp distinction between interpretation or understanding on the one hand and explanation on the other. The question asked and answered in interpretation or understanding is: 'What is this?' While in explanation the question asked and *explained* is 'Why this?' The explanation explains what there is (the facts). Moreover, understanding is connected with *intentionality* in a way explanation is not. There are mainly two kinds of explanations, namely causal and teleological. The causal explanation normally points to the past while teleological explanation always points to the future.

Before explanation can begin, its object, namely, *explanandum* must be described. Is there any room for genuine causal explanations in history? It would be imperative on my part to consider two main types of causal explanations, namely explanations in term of sufficient conditions, and explanations in term of necessary conditions before I answer this important but highly controversial question. It may not be out of place here to indicate, albeit briefly, the difference between sufficient condition and necessary condition. Suppose, p is a sufficient condition of q. Whenever p is, q will be there too. This means that the presence of p suffices to ensure the presence of q. On the other hand, p is a necessary condition of q means that whenever q is, p has to be there too, that is, the presence of q requires or presupposes the presence of p. The causal explanation in terms of sufficient conditions answers the question of the schematic form. *Why necessary*?, and the causal explanation in terms of necessary conditions answer the question of the type *how possible*? Causal explanations which look for sufficient conditions are not *directly* relevant to historical research. However, they may be *indirectly* relevant in two typical ways. One is when their *explananda* (states or events in the world) have interesting 'effects' on subsequent human affairs. The other is when their *explanantia* (states or events which are causally necessary for the existence of coming into being of the *explananda*) have interesting 'causes' in antecedent human actions and conditions.

A distinction between humean causes and humean effects on the one hand and a distinction between non-humean causes and non-humean effects on the other must be made in order to explicate the nature of causal explanation in history. Philosophers make a distinction between the relation of cause and effect on the one hand and distinction between the relation of ground and consequence on the other. The first is factual and empirical, the second conceptual and logical. David Hume, one of the great British empiricists and probably the greatest philosopher to write in English, makes the former distinction. For him, the relation between cause and effect is not one that of necessity but that of contingency since he advocates the regularity view of causation according to which the regularity that obtains between cause and effect has only an inductive base. He holds the view that cause and effect are nothing but brute facts. The humean view is that the causal relation that holds between brute facts, that is, cause and effect, is logically independent of one another. On the other hand, the non-humean view about the relation between cause and effect is contrary to that of the humean view since it holds that cause and effect are conceptually connected. And this view does not regard causes and effects as brute facts but as grounds and consequences respectively. According to the non-humean view, 'causes' in human affairs are very different from 'causes' of natural events, and that the notion of ground is essentially connected to the idea of human action in terms of motive, intention, inclination, disposition, and so on. This sort of causal explanation is quasi-teleological, for it explains *explanans* and *explanandum* in terms of human action and purpose. It must be noted here that the role of causal explanation proper is often to link the non-humean causes of its *explanans* with the non-humean effects of its *explanandum*. Thus, for example, if the destruction of a particular city was an act of envy or revenge on the part of a neighbouring city, and if the destruction in turn became an economic disaster for the entire region, it can be established that there is a connection between the rivalry of the two cities and subsequent changes in the economic life of the region. This is the kind of connection the historiographer is interested in. I would like to cite an instance from the history of North East India so as to focus this point a little more sharply. The Ahoms invaded the city of Dimapur with the explicit intention of expanding their kingdom. As a result, the city of Dimapur lost its level of civilisation, which it had achieved during the reign of the Kacharis. Thus it lost its pristine past glory.[3] It would be, therefore, reasonable to infer that the economic life of the whole city also deteriorated to a great extent. It can be established that there is a connection between the invasion of the Ahoms and the deterioration of the economic life of the whole city. The following schematic picture[4] may be used to bring out this point:

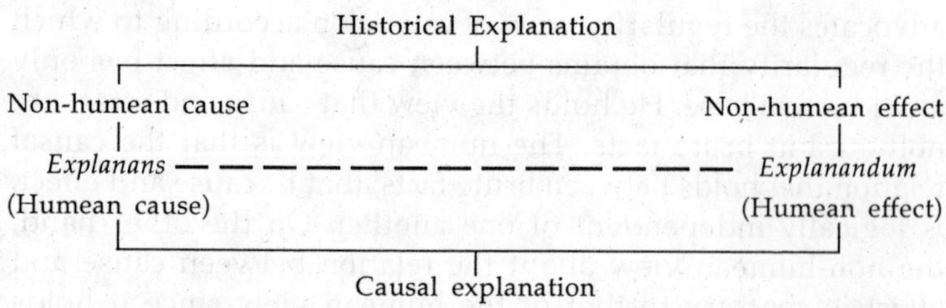

A somewhat different position is held in history by causal explanations of the *How possible*? type. For example, an archaeologist excavates a city and finds that big stones would be taken as an evidence that the people who lived in that city possessed some technological equipment or skill to transport these stones and raise them to their proper position in the wall. The possession of such a technological equipment or skill made it *causally possible* for them to achieve such feats. This explanation is genuinely causal since it depends for its validity on the existence of a nomic[5] connection. Let me take a leaf out of a book on the history of North East India to highlight the same point. Brick buildings erected at Rangpur by Rudra Singh, an Ahom King, in the 15th century A.D. serve as excellent evidence of the fact that advanced technology or skill was acquired during that time. These buildings have survived many an earthquake. These architectural wonders bear testimony to the fact that the mortar used to erect these buildings was of very high quality.[6] The ability to make such mortar made it *causally possible* for the Ahoms to achieve dizzy heights in the field of architecture. This explanation too is truly causal, since it also depends for its validity on the existence of a nomic connection. What relevance causal explanations of this kind have to historiography? In order for this kind of causal explanations to have any relevance at all, their *explananda* must be the results of individual or collective action. When this condition is fulfilled, the relevance of the explanation lies in its giving an answer to the question how *actions* were possible (not why they were undertaken). This is no longer in terms of *humean* causation. Therefore, my answer to the question, 'Is there any room for genuine causal explanation in history?' is an emphatic *yes*.

There are some difficulties, some real and some alleged, that plague the pursuit of historical knowledge. These are: (1) A historical discourse can never be an exhaustive account of what actually happened because it selects and abstracts from the concrete occurrences studied. This position leads to the wholesale scepticism concerning the possibility of 'objective' explanation in historical matters. (2) Historical inquiry is selective not only in its starting point; it is also selective in proposing solutions to its problems. A variety of sceptical doubts about the possibility of an ojective history has been expressed in consequence. One such doubt is based on the view that no account can render 'full reality' of what has occurred due to inexhaustibility of the numerous relations in which a given event stands to other events. Part of this doubt, that is, historical inquiry being selective in its starting point is selective in proposing solutions to its problems, can summarily be dismissed since unless an inquiry were selective it would never come near to resolving the specific question by which it is generated. This doubt also rests on another misconception, that is, it assumes that since every causal condition for an event has its own causal conditions, the event is never properly explained unless the entire regressive series of the latter conditions are also explained. There is no support for the claim that unless a series is terminated every proposed solution to a given problem is necessarily a distortion of the truth.

Every cognitive claim concerning matters of vital human interest is said to be valid only within the particular social setting in which it emerges, and the belief that it is possible to obtain explanations that are 'true' for everyone, irrespective of his position in a given society, is declared to be part of the self-deception of a culture because the historian is biased by his unconscious value orientations, his religious commitments, and his political leanings. This sort of scepticism raises three distinct issues. These are: (1) the choice of a particular problem for study, especially that inquires into human affairs, is undoubtedly controlled by the character of a given culture, sometimes by the status of that inquirer in that culture. However, this form of selective activity on the part of an inquirer does not necessarily jeopardize the objectivity of his findings. (2) No inquiry takes place in an intellectual vacuum, and every investigator approaches his task with information and guiding ideas derived in large measure from his culture. But it does not follow from the this that the value commitments of the investigator necessarily influence his acceptance of one conclusion rather than the other. In fact, there can be complete agreement among investigators despite their different social positions and loyalties. (3) The standards of validity operative in an inquiry are causally related to other cultural traits, and that social status, class and national bias, and general world perspectives more often than not influence what conclusion a man accepts. Biased thinking is a perennial challenge to the critical historian of human affairs: and research into causal determinants of bias is of great value of recognizing its occurrences and for mitigations, if not always eliminating its influences. This shows that objective explanation in history is not completely hopeless.

It must be noted here that though the radical scepticism rejects objective explanations of human affairs, it does concede the possibility of 'relational' type of objectivity because the investigators apply the same conceptual and *categorial* apparatus.

The search for explanations is directed to the ideal of ascertaining the necessary and sufficient conditions for the occurrence of phenomena. This ideal is rarely achieved even in the best-developed natural sciences. Most, if not all, historical inquiry is even further removed from this ideal due to the complexity and numorosity of the circumstances. Therefore, historians frequently cite only what they regard as the 'main', 'primary', 'principal', 'chief' or 'most important' causal factor. The truth of such statements is debatable, but none will say that they are without meaning. It is desirable, therefore, on the part of the historians to make explicit what such statements may be intended to convey.

Perhaps the most perplexing philosophical problem of history is this: can man, after all, achieve any sort of objective or verifiable knowledge about human affairs since his thoughts or judgements about its very nature, as well as his explanations of it, seem always to be coloured or distorted by his social status and objectives, what he wants and hopes to be the case? Some idealistic philosophers like Benedetto Croce[7] and R.G. Collingwood,[8] and more recently many an existentialist philosopher, have argued in the following manner. The historian deals with data which have meaning for him only in so far as he re-thinks and re-lives them in some emphathetic fashion or builds them into his own individual or social experience in some other way. Therefore, the historian does not achieve objective or scientific truth in the determination of facts since he picks and selects only the ones that have meaning or value for him and an understanding of which may help him solve his life problem. Moreover, these philosophers claim that historical interpretation of facts are myths, and not scientific explanations. A myth, they point out, however is not a falsehood but a value interpretation put upon the facts which has, for the historian who supplies the myth, and for others with his value orientation, the greatest truth possible. According to these thinkers, the same facts can be given different value interpretations, and thus conflicting myths emerge. For them history thus is constantly rewritten for every generation that departs, however, slightly, from the value orientation of the previous ones. It is no exaggeration to say that historical knowledge regarded this way turns out to be entirely relative.

It is true that history has to be rewritten so as to suit the aspirations and hopes of each generation. It must be noted here that this method belittles the importance of facts, and that it makes values entirely relative and subjective. This method is against the continuity of historical explanations. But the task of the historiographers is to maintain and preserve the continuity of historical inquiry so as to have a holistic account of such an inquiry. And this continuity sustains and preserves the relative objectivity of the historical enterprise without ignoring the significance of historical facts. Moreover, unless there is continuity in historical account, it would not be possible to discover or rediscover anything about the past. To sum up: I have tried to establish the following in this paper: (1) there is no radical difference between the explanations in natural sciences and the explanations in history, (2) there is room for genuine causal explanations in history, and these causal explanations are quasi-teleological in nature, (3) though absolute objectivity is not obtainable in history, it is possible to have relative objectivity in history, and (4) continuity in history is a must in order to discover or rediscover the truth about the past.

REFERENCES

1. W. Windelband, 'Geschichte and Natururssenchaft', Reprinted in, J.C.B. Mohr (ed.), Tubingen, 1907. Windelband Coined the label "nomothetic" for sciences which search for laws and "ideographic" for the descriptive study of individuality.
2. J.B. Bhattacharjee, *Pre-colonial North East India*, Har-Anand Publications in association with Vikas Publishing House Pvt. Ltd., 1991, p. 15.
3. *Ibid.*, pp. 137–138.
4. Georg Henrik Von Wright, *Explanations and Understanding*, Routledge and Kegan Paul, 1971, p. 137.
5. The term 'nomic' was suggested by W.E. Johnson. He says: "I should propose nomic should be substituted for necessary as contrasted with contingent. Thus a nomic proposition is that one expresses a pure law of Nature." *Logic*, 1934, Cambridge University Press, Chapters I–III.
6. J.B. Bhattacharjee, *op. cit.*, p. 137.
7. B. Croce, *La Storia Come Pension e come Azione*. Laterzal and Figli, Bari, 1938.
8. R.G. Collingwood, *An Essay on Metaphysics*, Oxford University Press, 1940.

CHAPTER 3

Objectivity and History: A Case Study of North East India

Let me begin with a few quotations. "Perhaps the most perplexing philosophical problem of history is this: can man, after all, achieve any sort of objective or verifiable knowledge about human affairs since his thoughts or judgements about its very nature, as well as his explanations of it, seem always to be coloured or distorted by his social status and objectives, what he wants and hopes to be the case?"[1] "It is true that history has to be rewritten so as to suit the aspirations and hopes of each generation. It must be noted here that this method belittles the importance of facts, and that it makes values entirely relative and subjective. This method is against the continuity of historical explanations. But the task of the historiographer is to maintain and preserve the continuity of historical inquiry so as to have a holistic account of such an inquiry. And this continuity sustains and preserves the relative objectivity of the historical enterprise without ignoring the significance of historical facts. Moreover, unless there is continuity in historical account, it could not be possible to discover or rediscover anything about the past."[2] "Though absolute objectivity is not obtainable in history, it is possible to have relative objectivity in history."[3] The primary aim of this chapter is to defend the view that relative objectivity (as opposed to absolute objectivity) is possible in history. In order to achieve the purpose of this paper, it is necessary to draw the attention to the historian's query as well as to state and reject eight criteria of absolute objectivity, which I propose do in the following way.

When a historian asks whether history can be objective, he does not suffer from any malady, especially from the malady of a generalized or epistemological scepticism. He is well aware of the fact that certain forms of enquiry such as physics can be conducted objectively. Therefore, his query is only whether or not the kind of objectivity that is obtainable in physics can be obtained in history.

Let us now consider eight criteria of objectivity in some detail so as to reject all of them as vacuous or empty or unintelligent or expressionless since they neither discriminate nor do they have any application.

Criterion One: (The Cartesian or mathematico-deductive): *An objective inquiry either (a) deduces its conclusions from self-evident axioms or (b) unfolds them from essences or definitions.* The historian could satisfy this cartesian criterion if and only if history consists in the gradual revelation of a plan, or an idea, as it has sometimes been held by the Hegelians. If it were the case, then history would become a science of pure thought like arithmetic, algebra, geometry, philosophy and logic, and historical investigation would be replaced by logical analysis. We can, therefore, safely conclude that if the 'objectivity' of a form of inquiry depends upon the possibility of deducing its content *a priori*, then history must abandon all claims to objectivity. However, the historian need not despair for the scientists also must have the same fate since they too cannot have any claim to this sort of objectivity.

Criterion Two: *An objective inquiry is one which begins from data which are literally such, that is, which nakedly confront us.* This criterion was advocated by Ernst Mach, a physicist. The nineteenth century historians were to a great extent attracted by this criterion. But they found it impossible to apply this criterion for the following two important reasons:

(1) Since events which concern the historian are past, there cannot be 'data which are literally such', but must always be inferences or reconstructions. (2) The natural scientists can

always pass beyond the recorded facts to the facts themselves. And this ability to have direct reference to facts is considered to be the essence of objectivity according to this criterion. The scientist can confront the world as it nakedly is. On the other hand, the historian cannot confront the world as it nakedly is for the simple reason that he sees the world always through the medium of some one else's testimony. And a testimony by its very nature cannot be passed beyond because events the testimony describes are gone for ever. Moreover, if the scientist doubts the testimony of some other scientist that when hydrochloric acid is passed on zinc, hydrogen is produced, he can repeat the experiment for himself. This cannot be done by the historian. This criterion, therefore, leads to the disturbing conclusion that the historian cannot achieve objectivity. The historian, however, need not unduly worry about this for the simple reason that he is not trying to achieve this sort of objectivity.

***Criterion Three**: An objective inquiry is a direct examination of the world which does not rely upon testimony.* Even some historians subscribe to this criterion for they have a preference for what 'they can see with their own eyes'. These historians are obviously mistaken for the following reason. The historians can take a wider view of the situation than is accessible to any direct participant. It must be also borne in mind that the historians do not in fact go in search of 'old soldiers'. Moreover, there is nothing 'non-objective' about using of testimony unless 'obejective' is vacuous. However, this does not mean that any particular testimony is exempted from critical examination.

There is no denying the fact that historians do occasionally have to depend upon only chronicles, or in the worst case, on a single chronicle.[4] But even then they are not quite at the mercy of the chronicler. They have their own ways of testing chronicle accounts. Moreover, they can discover important facts by their methods of testing, which the chronicles had no intention. In short, historians need not rely on the propaganda of partisans.

***Criterion Four**: The statements must 'mean the same' for all observers.* This criterion of objectivity can be rejected out right by saying that it makes objectivity vacuous. It is true that historical statements have degrees of 'open texture'. But this does not mean that they are 'subjective'.

Criterion Five: *An inquiry is objective only if it keeps to atomic facts.* This criterion implies that historians impose relations and connections upon facts, which are quite devoid of them. This sort of implication is reminiscent of the British empiricist view that all relations are 'the work of the mind'. But relations and connections are ingredients within the simplest facts. Therefore, there is no *a priori* reason for maintaining that order is imposed, as distinct from discovered.

Criterion Six: *An inquiry is objective only if it does not select from within its material.* It is a fact that historians regard certain facts as unimportant and others as important. It means that he distinguishes between these two sorts of facts. According to some scholars, this sort of selection of materials makes historical inquiries subjective. Descartes echos the same kind of complaint in his *Discourse on Method* (Part-I). I quote: "If they do not wholly misrepresent or exaggerate the value of things in order to render them worthy of being read, at least omit in them all the circumstances which are basset and least notable; and from that fact it follows that what is retained is not portrayed as it really is".[5] *Prima facie,* this is a queer criterion, because every form of inquiry is selective. However, there is more to this criticism than it meets the eye, which is as follows. Let it be granted that there are historical facts, let it be also granted that these facts are 'important' or 'unimportant' in relation to a particular reconstruction, even then history fails to be objective because there are no grounds on which one historical reconstruction can rationally be preferred to another. This objection is not as decisive as it appears to be for there are grounds or reasons available to historian to rationally prefer one reconstruction to another.[6]

Criterion Seven: *A branch of inquiry is objective only if it contains* a method of deciding between conflicting hypotheses. Popper in his book *The Open Society and Its Enemies* argues that history does not satisfy this criterion. His criticism boils down to this: the hypotheses of history are *ad hoc* hypotheses, and we are free to choose as we like between *ad hoc* hypotheses. The historian is not *constrained* by the facts since all the relevant facts are already before him when he constructs his hypotheses.

Popper's argument, however, ignores the fact that historical hypotheses do lead to revisions of accepted views.[7] Nevertheless, in history there is *sometimes* no known way of deciding between historical hypotheses. But this difficulty is not peculiar to history and therefore ought not to be levelled against its objectivity.

***Criterion Eight**: In objective inquiries, conclusions are universally acceptable.* This perhaps is the most popular of all grounds for denying the objectivity of history. The core of this criterion is this: the cases of history and natural science do not seem to be parallel. One distinguishes a Roman Catholic from a Protestant historian. One distinguishes a Marxist interpretation from a non-Marxist interpretation of an important historical event. But we do not have these sorts of distinctions as far as natural science is concerned. In other words, this is to say that historical explanations are beset with prejudices, biases and unscientific methods.I am entirely in agreement with Passmore when he says, "If the test of objectivity is that there are regular ways of settling issues, by the use of which men of whatever party can be brought to see what actually happened, then I do not see how one can doubt the objectivity of history. But if we are satisfied with nothing less than the production of histories which all men the least material will accept as final, then that would be a greater victory for the scientific spirit than we have any reason to expect. Such unanimity, however, is not to be found in any branch of human inquiry. Once again, if we press the criterion of objectivity too hard, it applies to no form of inquiry; slacken it slightly and history edges its way in with the rest."[8]

After having rejected the above mentioned eight criteria for objectivity, I would now like to give the ninth criterion, which I subscribe to.

***Criterion Nine**: History has 'relative' objectivity, which is sustained and preserved by the continuity of historical inquiry without ignoring the significance of historical facts.* First of all, I would like to spell out what I exactly mean by the term 'relative' lest I am misunderstood. I do not mean subjective by 'relative'. What I am trying to do is to draw a distinction between what I call 'absolute objectivity' and 'relative objectivity' or between vacuous objectivity and non-vacuous objectivity. This makes it clear that by 'relative objectivity' I mean non-vacuous objectivity. I have maintained[9] that the task of historiographer is to maintain and preserve the continuity of historical inquiry so as to have a holistic account of such an inquiry.[10] I am convinced that history is capable of achieving this purpose by adopting the ninth criterion. It is worth reiterating that this criterion does not ignore the significance of historical facts. It is no exaggeration to say that facts are objective by being public.

REFERENCES

1. S.C. Daniel, "The Logic of Historical Analysis: Reflections on North-Eastern Historiography", *Proceedings of North East India History Association*, Twelfth Sessions, Jagi Road, 1991, edited and published by Jayanta Bhusan Bhattacharjee, Shillong (India), p. 25.
2. *Ibid.*, p. 26.
3. *Ibid.*
4. It is a well known fact that chronicles have been used as source-material for writing the history of Ahom period. It is also a well known fact that *Buranjis* (Ahom Chronicles) contain enormous historical data. However, these data must be used judiciously and after sufficient cross verification. Some historians are guilty of limiting the scope of historical enquiry by using only these Chronicles ignoring the importance of other available historical data.
5. Rene Descartes, *A Discourse on Method*. Translated by John Veitch, Everyman's Library, London, J.M. Dent and Sons Ltd., 1949.
6. Many historians of North-East India have worked on similar area of research, and from almost the same materials. And yet their researches have often different conclusions. Some, for instance, such as Amalendu Guha have given a Marxist interpretation (refer to *Planter Raj to Swaraj – Freedom Struggle and Electoral Politics in Assam 1826–1947*, People's Publishing House, New Delhi, 1988) while H.K. Barpujari has given a non-Marxist interpretation. (Refer to three volumes of *Political History of Assam*, Government of Assam, Dispur, Gauhati, 1978–1980). The above mentioned historians do have their grounds or reasons to rationally prefer one interpretation to another.
7. There are instances available in the writings of the history of North-East India where historians have revised their earlier views. For example, H.K. Barpujari did not express an explicit appreciation of the rule of American missionaries in North-East India in his earlier works

on Assam. He is highly appreciative of the same in *The American Missionaries and North-East India (1836–1990 A.D.),* (Spectrum Publication, Gauhati-Delhi, 1986). He dedicates his book as follows: "To the hallowed memory of those Christian missionaries whose ceaseless toil and dedication had received and modernised the Assamese language and literature and paved the way for Renaissance in Assam at the close of the last century."

8. J.A. Passmore, "The Objectivity of History", in *Philosophical Analysis and History,* (ed.) William II. Dray, Harper and Row, New York and London, 1966.
9. S.C. Daniel, op. cit., p. 26.
10. Some historians of North-East India have tried to maintain and preserve The Continuity of historical inquiry so as to have a holistic account of such an inquiry. Refer to *History and Culture of the Cavos* (M. Sangma, Books Today, New Delhi, 1981) and to *The Khasi Canvas* (J.N. Choudhury, Shillong, 1978).

CHAPTER 4

Hume's Theory of History: A Conspectus

(David Hume, 1711–1776)

David Hume is one of the greatest British philosophers, and probably, one of the greatest philosophers in the entire history of Western philosophy. Hume's philosophy has provoked extreme responses from philosophers in the West since the publications of his *Magnum Opus, A Treatise of Human Nature*. Some consider him to be an exceptional genius, and some, unfortunately, dismiss him as a mere Sophist. But none can afford to ignore his contribution to the progress of philosophy. His historical works include *History of England* and two long essays on "The Populousness of Ancient Nations", and "Of the Study of History"; the "Natural History of Religion" is also, in the main, an historical work. Hume's *History of England* became a popular work. Also, it was the first important historical work in English and the first comprehensive history of Britain in any language. V.C. Chapell has the following to say about this work. He says: "It has long since been superseded as history, although it remained a standard work for nearly a century, but is till worth reading for its style."[1] I would like to differ slightly from the view of V.C. Chapell by saying that it is not only worth reading for its style, but also for its historical content. Very little work has been done on Hume's theory of history in modern times, especially on his important essay, "Of the Study of History". This chapter is an attempt to critically examine Hume's theory of history as explicated in, "Of the Study of History", and to make it relevant in the context of the historical writings in North-East India.

Let me start with a quotation. Hume eulogizes history with the following words: "I must add, that history is not only a valuable part of knowledge, but opens the door to many other parts, and affords materials to most of the sciences. And indeed, if we consider the shortness of human life, and our limited knowledge, even of what passes in our own time, we must be sensible that we should be forever children in understanding, were it not for the invention, which extends our experiences to all past ages, and to the most distant nations; making them contribute as much to our improvement in wisdom, as they had actually lain under our observations. A man acquainted with history may, in some respect, be said to have lived from the beginning of the world, (and to *have been making continual additions to his stock of knowledge in every century*)[2]

Here, we find the historian given the role of a quarter master, stocking materials for the serious scientific campaigns for the future. More revealing is Hume's "addition theory of knowledge", according to which changing theories and ideas result in an addition to, but not an alteration of, mankind's conception of what knowledge itself is. Needless to say that this "addition theory of knowledge" is worth considering. While considering this, I would like to examine just two historical theories so as to relate them to the North-East India historical scenario. And these two main theories are: (i) Particularism, and (ii) Universalisation. This is not to say that there are no other important theories. As a matter of fact, there are, such as the theories of G. Vico, I. Kant, K.R. Popper, and so many others. I would like to give an exposition of the above mentioned two theories, namely, Particularism and Universalisation albeit very succintly.

Particularism is a theory that experience rather than reason is the source of knowledge. This general thesis, however, can receive different emphases and refinements. One such emphasis and refinement connects particularism and inductivism. And this sort of emphasis and refinement is specially applicable to history. It is a truism to say that inductivism deals with non-demonstrative arguments. In this type of arguments, the truth of the premises, while not entailing the truth of the conclusion, purports to be a good reason for belief in it. And these arguments may be called 'ampliative' because of the fact that the conclusion may presuppose the existence of individuals whose existence is not presupposed by the premises. Sceptics may question the validity of the "ampliativeness" of inductive argument or empirical method adopted by certain historians. In my opinion, the question is entirely misplaced, for no one can expect a necessary or universal conclusion from an inductive argument or empirical method. In other words, it is absurd to except a non-empirical conclusion from empirical premise (s). However, inductive argument or empirical method is not completely bereft of any logical force. In fact, it has tremendous logical force. And this logical force consists in the following. The inductive or empirical conclusion is often based on overwhelming evidences, and sometimes on not so overwhelming evidences. The conclusion thus reached has the logic force of indicating powerfully that anything contrary to it will be most probably false.

How to understand human history? Either there is only one history, that is, history of mankind, or there are histories of communities, societies, and groups. The universalists claim that there is only one history, that is, the history of mankind, and the histories of particular groups and communities are imperfect manifestations of that universal one.

The particularists, on the other hand, claim that universal history is a myth. It may be a kind of generalization of particular histories. The universal history takes into account only the so called *Geist* or Spirit or Soul, and according to it, history is created when the *Geist* moves, and this is a well defined path and well-ordained goal which the *Geist* has to travel and achieve. This process is purely rational and logical and hence the process cannot be changed or altered or modified. It can be either delayed or accelerated. On the other hand, the particularists claim that the history is made by people (charismatic individuals), nations and communities. The universalists discover universal, inevitable, impersonal, and immovable forces or laws of historical development. It is worth noting that the idealists lay emphasis on the spiritual process, and the materialists lay emphasis on material, economic forces. But both the groups travel in the same boat, probably, in different corners.

Further, the universalists may adopt either linear approach or cyclical approach. Ancient Indian historiographers as well as modern western historiographers like O. Spangler and Arnold Toynbee adopt cyclical approach. For them, there is no such thing as historical period of time; time is eternity. For the linearist, the history moves from a particular period of time to another. Hegel, Marx and many others adopt this view of understanding human history.

Let us try to understand and reconstruct the history of North-East India in the light of these historiographical models. I wish to propose a synthetic model (a compromise between particularism and universalism) with certain appropriate modifications.

By history, Hume does not mean political or social history alone. By history, he means the history of mankind. In other words, it is the history of what man has done; what he has created. The exhaustive of this totality is history for Hume. In this sense, though the historians are born accidentally in a particular period of time, yet he relives and re-experiences all the experiences of his ancestors and anticipates the future. In this sense, history is the history of human nature. Though Hume is a particularist in epistemology, yet he seems to be inclined towards universalism in history for the simple reason that he advocates "the addition theory of knowledge", according to which knowledge is a totality, nothing is lost sight of, nothing is ignored.

It may not be out of place to give a brief outline of Hume's epistemology and metaphysics so as to understand his deviation as regards history. Hume holds the view that we cannot have certain knowledge as far as the matters of fact are concerned. He says that reason is a kind of cause and truth is its effect. But, reason as the cause cannot produce its effect due to the influence of other causes and the limited mental powers. He comes to the conclusion that knowledge degenerates into probability due to these reasons. Hume says that it is impossible to find out when knowledge ends and probability begins. He is of the view that knowledge and probability are contradictory and diametrically opposed to one another. When knowledge is present, probability will be absent, and *vice-versa*. Our judgements being founded only on probability, are always followed by uncertainty and doubt. Hume has the following theory of probability. The evidence of our judgement of matters of fact is probable and followed by a doubt. The second judgement will be weakened by the second doubt, the third by the third doubt and so on *ad infinitum*. As a result, at the end there will be nothing but a total extinction of belief and evidence.

Hume holds the view that sceptic must believe in the existence of body or matter, though he cannot maintain its veracity by philosophical arguments. He has no choice — the nature has not left the belief in the existence of body or matter to his choice. Nature (human nature) thinks that it is too important an issue to be left to our 'uncertain reasoning and speculation'. Hume asks the following philosophically important and oft quoted question. Hume says: "We may well ask, what causes induce us to believe in the existence of body? But 'tis in vain to ask, whether there be body or not?"[3] Hume holds the view that we do not perceive any apart from our impressions or perceptions. He refuses to go beyond the veil of impressions or perceptions. This is his brand of atomism. He does not believe in the existence of body or matter.

Hume also denies the existence of self or mind. He says that some philosophers are of the view that we are conscious of our self or mind every moment. These philosophers are also of the view that perfect identity and simplicity of the self are very certain, and that they are beyond the evidence of demonstration. These philosophers come to the conclusion that if the existence of the self is dubious, then, we cannot be certain about anything at all. Hume says that unfortunately all these assertions are contrary to the facts of experiences. We cannot have any idea of the self since we cannot have an impression of the same. The question, 'From what impression could this idea be derived?' cannot be answered. If we try to answer this question, we will land ourselves in contradictions and absurdities. But, an answer is necessary to make the idea of the self clear and intelligible. The self or person does not consist of just one impression, but it consists of many impressions and ideas. If any one impression gives rise to the idea of the self, it must continue to exist invariably the same since the self is supposed to exist in that way. But, no impression is constant and invariable; all the impressions are interrupted and thus discontinuous. Therefore, no impression can give rise to the idea of the self. Hume says, "For my part, when I enter most intimately into what I call *myself*, I always stumble on some particular perception or other, of heat or cold, light or shade, love or hatred, pain or pleasure. I never can catch *myself* at any time without a perception, and never can observe anything but the perception. When my perceptions are removed for any time, as by sound sleep; so long am I insensible of myself, and may truly be said not to exist. And were all my perceptions removed by death, and could I neither think, nor feel, nor see, nor love, nor hate after the dissolution of my body, I should be entirely annihilated, nor do I conceive what is farther requisite to make me a perfect non-entity."[4] He is certain that there is no such principle as simple and continued self, at least in himself.

Hume's arguments for the non-existence of the self can be equally applied to his proof for the non-existence of God. Since there cannot be any impression of God, he argues, there cannot be any genuine idea of the same. According to him, God did not create man, but man has created God, and God is a figment of man's imagination.

It is extremely strange that Hume being a particularist in his epistemology, meta-physics and philosophy of religion, adopts a universalistic approach to his theory of history.

Appendix

J.B. Bhattacharjee, one of the foremost historians of North-East India, seems to uphold universalism. In his Presidential Address to the Fourteenth Session of North-East India History Association, held at Jorhat in 1993, he indicates that the 'immediate task before the historians of North-East India is to develop a north-eastern perspective of historical analysis so as to identify the priority areas and adopt an appropriate action plan. In his view, the topmost priority is to have a proper perspective of history as an applied academic discipline and its thorough reorientation in that direction. In this connection, he has the following to say, "The old notion that history is just a study of the past is doomed to destruction. History is, in effect, a science of study in retrospect; it is a *process* and a *continuity* (italics are mine). It is not the study of the past for past's sake; its concern is the present and the future of the society. It is not a study of the past that is behind the society: *history's past is living and moving in shaping the future* (again, the italics are mine)"[5] The above quoted passage amply proves that J.B. Bhattacharjee is committed to universalistic approach *vis a vis* history. Since the quoted passage is self-explanatory, I am not offering any explanation of my own.

D.R. Syiemlieh, one of the very promising historians of North-East India, adopts the theory of Particularism at times. Refer to his articles, "The Robert Lindsay Muniments",[6] "The Beginning of the Catholic Church among the Mizos",[7] and "Thomas Jones' "Injudicious Marriage?"[8] This, however, does not mean that D.R. Syiemlieh does not adopt universalistic approach to analyse historical events.

REFERENCES

1. V.C. Chapell, *The Philosophy of David Hume*, Random House Inc., 1963, pp. x & xi.
2. David Hume, "Of the Study of History", *The Philosophical Works of David Hume*, Ed., T.H. Greene and T.H. Grosse, London: Longmans, Green and Co., 1898, iv, 390.
3. David Hume, *A Treatise of Human Nature*, Ed., L.A. Selby-Biggs, p. 183.
4. *Ibid.*, p. 252.
5. J. B. Bhattacharjee, Presidential Address, *Proceedings of North East India History Association, Fourteenth Session*, Jorhat, 1993, Kamala Art Press, Shillong, p. 2.
6. David R. Syiemlieh, "The Robert Lindsay Muniments", *Proceedings of North East India History Association, Twelfth Session*, Jagi Road, 1991, Kamala Art Press, Shillong, pp. 90–100.
7. David R. Syiemlieh, "The Beginning of the Catholic Church among the Mizos", *The Proceedings of North East India History Association, Thirteenth Session*, Shillong, 1993, Kamala Art Press, Shillong, pp. 273-278.
8. David R. Syiemlieh, *The Proceedings of North East India History Association, Fifteenth Session*, Doimukh, 1994, Modern Offset, Shillong, pp. 240-244.

CHAPTER 5

Kant's Philosophy of History: A Conspectus

(Immanuel Kant, 1724–1804)

This chapter makes an attempt to reconstruct Kant's philosophy of history as systematically as possible. Needless to point out that metaphysics and moral history are very closely related to each other in Kant's architectonic. Kant is of the firm conviction that moral — historical ideal is an effective means of giving a justification for the very existence of the world and its 'final end'. He also considers history as an essential, albeit problematic, aspect of critical philosophy. This article will examine the following basic tenets of Kant's philosophy of history, namely (1) History of Reason, (2) History as the Moral Totality, and (3) The History of Philosophy and its Architectonic. This article will therefore consist of three parts, and also of an appendix, wherein the relevance of Kant's Philosophy of History for the historical writings on North-East India, will be highlighted.

Part I – History of Reason

Is rationalism compatible with the modern historical outlook? This question has not been answered by the rationalists of the Englightenment. The modern successors of the Enlightenment have attempted to answer this significant question in a very serious and sincere manner. It must be pointed out here that the philosophers of the Age of Reason such as Plato, Descartes, Spinoza and Leibniz saw reason as eternal, unchangeable, non-temporal, and not restricted by cultural and sociological factors. Consequently, history was considered to be a contingent, empirical enterprise, without rational ingredient in itself consisting of simple accumulation or presenting facts that *per se* neither unfold a rational order nor are relevant to the growth of rationality. According to this view of history, in a nutshell, individual man belonged to *the world of becoming* while reason 'itself' was a *pure being*, static and permanent.

The newly conceived historicism of the eighteenth century challenged the above mentioned ancient view. The problem was to admit the rational significance of history as well as to provide it with a systematic *ground*. Needless to say that this indicated an reevaluation of the nature and status of history. For history to have a rational significance, reason itself must be interpreted in such a way so as to allow for its possible historization.

Kant tried to remove the antagonism between rationalism and historicism. Even though he was concerned with the pure and transcendental forms of human reason, he did not consider them as fixed and given, but as *constituted* by the rational subject. He thus introduced what may be called his "Copernican revolution of rationality" — a revolution that has a telling bearing on his view of the nature of reason as well as his new doctrines of epistemology and metaphysic of morals. This revolution refused to accept the Platonic model of reason and suggested the systematic ground that could fundamentally account for the historization of reason. In fact, Hegel's theory depended on the same basic revolution. Reason, for Hegel, has a *becoming*, because it is the product of the rational subject, who has constituted himself through his historical development. The anti-Platonic theory of rationality was thus logically necessary for Hegel's concept of a history of reason. But on this crucial point, Hegel did not invent an absolutely new principle: he only developed more coherently and comprehensively an idea that Kant had already expressed implicitly and without explicitly stating the art or practice of examining statements logically, as by question and answer, to establish validity.

Kant introduces a very clear concept of a "history of reason", a history that is itself rational or "transcendental" and not empirical. It permeates throughout his philosophy of ethics and religion; it underlies his theory of scientific revolutions and his history of philosophy; and it has its systematic roots in his meta-philosophy. There is no doubt that there is a *prima facie* legitimacy of his concept of a history of reason. Given this *prima facie* legitimacy, we can ask two questions about it, namely, (i) *quid facti* (as a matter of fact), and (ii) *quid juris* (as a matter of principle). (i) *The History of Reason: Quid Facti*: Generally speaking, the history of reason has two main plainly apparent things in Kant: one is the history of reason reshaping the *world*, and the other is the history of reason becoming known and explained to itself. The first aspect of the history of reason is mainly practical; it is the process whereby human reason stamps itself upon the actual world, reshaping its empirical organization in light of its own goals and interests. In this practical sense, rational history is an *open-ended* process, moving towards an infinite distant ideal. The sense of the history of reason is mainly theoretical (using 'theory' in the broad sense, including theory of morality); it is the process whereby human reason gradually explains its dormant pattern, manifesting its main concepts, principles, and interests within a logical order and connection. This aspect of the history of reason in principle is *finite*; it leads to scientific revolutions, which raise the varied theoretical disciplines like logic, mathematics, physics, and eventually philosophy itself to the level of valid science, and thus, in fact, *abolish* their history and give them a final, unchangeable form. Let me elaborate a little on each aspect of the history of reason. (1) *The History of Praxis*: Kant was interested in history primarily as a moral task rather than as a cognitive object. History is the field of action in which human action is supposed to create a progressive synthesis between the moral demands of reason (practical reason) and the world of experience (phenomenal world). This synthesis should not be confined to singular acts and particular results, but should cover the whole range of human practical experience. Thus, it must serve as a principle of *totalization*, gradually changing the basic shapes of the moral, political, and cultural world.

Kant calls the highest totality towards which the process is oriented, "the highest good in the world". To make coherent sense, this rational ideal should be seen as the regulative idea of history; and correspondingly, Kant's special imperative or command, "Act to promote the highest good in the world", can properly be called the historical imperative. On the other hand, the rational goal of the highest good, that is, the total moral end of humanity, also expresses the supreme interest of reason; and thus rational history is not only woven into Kant's critical system, but even related to its very architectonic, (2) *The History of Theory*: The concept of a history of reason in Kant's system is to be found in the process by which human reason realizes the theoretical potential and becomes known and explicated to itself. This includes the history of the sciences, especially of philosophy. Kant conceives of reason as an interested or "erotic" activity moving towards a systematic explication of itself. Underlying this process is a latent paradigm ("schema") that all philosophical systems have been gradually achieving: All the important doctrines in the history of philosophy are thereby implied members of one systematic whole, each narrowly stressing some particular "interest of reason" and special aspects of the final pure system. This one-sidedness produces antinomies or contradictions among the historical system, leading to their breakdown. However, the collapse of historical systems leaves out an immense multitude of particular concepts, principles, and categories, which gradually add up until they find a new systematic organization. According to Kant, this process is finite; like. the other theoretical sciences, philosophy is expected to undergo a final *revolution*, creating the ultimate system, which removes the antinomies or contradictions among historical systems and finally actualizes the latent paradigm of reason in full. This revolution will, for the first time, make philosophy a science, which will end its historical process in which one can only philosophize and not yet 'learn philosophy' since the final system does away philosophy as the love of knowledge and makes it into actual knowledge. Some passages from Kant's chapter on Architectonic in his frist Critique, that is, *Critique of Pure Reason*, present a first hand impression of Kant's idea of the history of reason. For instance, he says: "Systems seem to be formed in the manner of lowly organisms, through a *generated acquivoca* from the mere confluence of assembled concepts, at first imperfect, and only gradually attaining to completeness, although they, one and all have had their schema, on the original germ, in the sheer self-development of reason."[1]

In summary, Kant presents reason as showing development and a historical goal. It gradually becomes explained or known to itself in a progressive movement, and it is also expected to modify the actual world according to its precepts and practical goals, then promoting the highest good. From these perspectives, the concept of rational history not only belongs to the critical philosophy but also to the highest good. And around the supreme goal the whole system is architectonically organized.

The History of Reason: Quid Juris

In order to understand Kant's conception of reason, it is necessary to mention its three main sources. One in Kant's discussion of the "Architectonic[2] of Human Reason", an important source for understanding his meta-philosophy. The second source is Kant's principle of the Copernican revolution, which needs to be explicated in his ontology, ethics and aesthetics. The third source is Kant's many symbolic representations to the functions, interests, tasks, and even "needs" and "aspirations" of human reason that pervade the main parts of his writings. Kant conceives of reason mainly as a spontaneous activity, not as a mere set of Forms or Ideas like Plato. Even the objective side of reason, that is, its concepts, principles and the like, must be seen as subjective functions, by which the human mind or ego structures itself as well as its experience. This *dynamic* conception of reason is radically different from that of Plato. In fact, this novel conception breaks away from the whole classic view of the *logos* as fixed and independent, governing the mind and the world as a thing-in-itself. For Kant, whatever is rational depends on the thinking subject. Reason cannot be separated from the actual operation of thinking or form the practical attitudes of the mind but is formed by them while also forming them. Thus, the very status of rationality is not ready made but constituted, which depends on the spontaneous activity of the ego, and this supplies a systematic ground for assigning reason a "becoming" of its own. This becoming must, moreover, assume: a specifically historical character because of the finitude of human reason. As finite, human reason is necessarily confronted with the problem of its own historization. Since it is finite, there is a difference between the possible and the actual. It means that there is a gap between its limited potential and its actual articulations. And then the finite human reason confronts the problem or the task of gradually closing this gap. The reason must be actualized in a progressive move of self-explication; and thus, human reason is contingent on a history and a becoming of its own.

Part II – History as the Moral Totality

A reinterpretation of the highest good (*sommum bonum*) will lead to the view that the highest good is the regulative idea of history. A reevaluation of the highest good in the light of the idea of history is also a reinterpretation of the idea of history as an integral part of the critical philosophy. The highest good remains a "synthesis" of moral and empirical elements, but not of virtue and happiness alone, but of "freedom" and "nature" at large; and to achieve it now means to imprint the demands of the moral idea upon the whole gamut or totality of an empirical environment, changing the patterns of our psychological disposition, our social and political institutions, as well as the surrounding physical and ecological systems—insofar as they relate to the sphere of human needs and moral interests. These changes are due partly to logical requirements implied in Kant's point of deviation, and partly to his departure of interest. The "synthesis" thus understood allow us to see the highest good, in Kantian terms as the regulative idea of history, actually as the end concept that defines it. History is the process in which the highest good should be realized, and in which the free, formative activity of practical reason transforms the given world into a new, moral world. The historical end also serves as a focal point which unifies or "totalizes" the intentions and actions of all individual moral agents and all areas of collective creativity such as law, politics and education. History is thus the process when the required "synthesis" of freedom and nature should occur. Moreover, Kant attributes to reason a metaphysical interest striving for the absolute and the total. Having been denied fulfilment in the field of knowledge, it now finds positive satisfaction in the field of moral-historical action. The result of the whole critical system is to carry the metaphysical interest, in its quest for ultimates and totalities, from the deviant cognitive path to its expression in moral history. Thus the ideas of the highest good and history, far from being marginal, becomes the systematic apex of Kant's whole critical enterprise. It must be shown that the concept of the highest good, in all its meanings, defines the boundaries of the second stage of Kant's philosophy of practice, lying beyond the formal ethics of the categorical imperative. It means that though Kant's practical philosophy is based upon the theory of the categorical imperative, it is not completed by it. Of the crucial importance is the dialectic of practical reason, or the doctrine of the postulates and the highest good, that compliments the formal ethics with a material element and presents human practice with its ultimate objective. Kant's practical system should be then divided into two parts or stages, the formal and the material, or is Kant's terminology, the absolute and the comprehensive, or the unconditioned and the whole (total). The first stage is discussed in his book, *Foundations of the Metaphysics of Morals.*[3] It examines the structure of the good and establishes its absolute principle, including the negative and positive freedom of the will, its special power of motivation, the universal form which governs its legislation, and also the subjective initiative of the moral agent in formulating this law by acting in accordance with it. The second stage, on the other hand, fulfils the need "to conceive some sort of final and for all our actions and abstentions, takes as a whole".[4] It does not merely determine the absolute principle of the moral will but goes on to define the *total object*. Its pivot is the formulation of a new imperative with a definite content, that is, to act to promote the highest good in the world. To Kant, it would be a more complete and comprehensive imperative than the basic categorical one. The latter (the basic categorical one) tells us *how* to act, while the former (a more complete and comprehensive imperative) tells us in addition *what* should be realized, as the final outcome of moral actions. It is concerned not with the specific "what" of particular actions, which obviously depends on contingent circumstances, but only with that fixed, total object to which all moral actions should ultimately aspire. Thus, it responds to the double 'need of reason', namely: (1) the *logical* requirement of reason that the sphere of action be "totalized", that is, systematized synoptically; and (2) a *subjective* or psychological condition of the human mind, to "our rational needs" as humans, since "in the absence of all reference to an end, no determination of the will can take place in man."[5]

As far as the Highest Good is concerned, there are four major groups of definitions. First: "virtue and happiness together constitute the possession of the highest good for one person."[6] Here, the highest good has a personal meaning. It is the highest good of *somebody*. The moral constituent is described as virtue (*Tugond*), which is a characteristic of an individual, and the happiness is his private happiness. Second: "[This *summum bonum* is formed by] the union of the greatest welfare of the rational beings in the world with the supreme condition of their good, or, in other words, (by) the union of universal happiness with strictest moralisty."[7] Here, the highest good appears as a *universal* system of morality and reward, which includes all of humanity. It is an idea that unifies the ends of all possible *wills*. Third: It is a broader view of the highest good, as "the union of the purposiveness arising from freedom with the purposiveness of nature."[8] *Fourth*: The harmony of experience and morality should be created by human action. And this can be done only by human action. And also, this can be done only by man's reshaping of the sensuous world in light of a supersensuous idea, and by his creating new social and ecological system. This sort of moral nature suggests the idea of history.

Part III – The History of Philosophy and Its Architectonic

It must be pointed out that Kant's relationship to the history of philosophy, on the whole, is not scholarly but philosophical. He is keenly aware of the *historically* of *philosophy in general* and of the special place that his own system is to occupy within it. The nature of this place is twofold. On the one hand, Kant sees his system as a continuation no less than as a radical change. His revolution relies on the previous history of philosophy not only for its particular materials, but also equally for its philosophical programme and its new systematic grounding. On the other hand, Kant's system is to *overcome* the historicality of philosophy and brings it process to a close. Through it, human reason will become completely explained and known to itself and the series of past opinions will result in a philosophical *science*. Following the example of logic, mathematics, and the natural sciences, Kant's revolution is to change philosophy from historicised *doxa* or belief into pure and timeless *episteme* or knowledge, and then to transcend or go beyond its history.

Kant thus had a strong sense both of the historical nature of philosophy and of the new, trans-historical era that was emerging. Even before Hegel, he was the first philosopher of the "end of philosophy" in the *historical* sense of the word. Prior to him, almost all philosophers considered that their works had reached the final truth, because they were convinced that the history of previous philosophy was accidental, a contingent series of errors and opinions, unessential to the emergence of truth through their own work. Kant, on the other hand, places his revolution at the end of a necessary process of gradual unfolding, a process that has made his own system possible and has been sustained and systematized by it. Kant's philosophy is the conclusion and overcoming of the inevitable historization of reason, its need to undergo a *process* of self explication.

It is worth noting that Kant ends his first critique with his much cherished hope. He says: "As regards those who adopt *a scientific* method, they have the choice of method, they have the choice of proceeding either *dogmatically* or sceptically; but in any case they are under obligation to proceed *systematically*. I may cite the celebrated Wolff as a prepresentative of the former mode of procedure, and David Hume as a representative of the latter, and may then, conformably with my present purpose, leave all other unnamed. The *critical* path done is still open. If the reader has had the courtesy and patience to accompany me along this path, he may now judge for himself, if he cares to lend his aid in making this path with a high road, it may not be possible to achieve before the end of the present century what many centuries have not been able to accomplish; namely, to secure for human reason complete satisfaction in regard to that with which it has all along so eagerly occupied itself, though hitherto in vain."[9] It is possible to discern a theory of history, albeit in sketchy manner, in Kant after a careful and thorough examination.

It is worth noting that my reconstruction of Kant's theory of history is based on his chapters on "The History of Pure Reason", of first critique, that is, *Critique of Pure Reason*. Kant includes his theory of history of reason in his system of reason itself, and incorporates it in his meta-philosophy framework.

Kant says: "Systems seem to be formed in the manner of lowly organisms, though a *generatio aequivoca* form the mere confluence of assembled concepts, at first imperfect, and only gradually attaining to completeness, although they one and all have had their schema, as the original germ in the sheer self-development of reason. Hence, not only in each system articulated in accordance with the idea, but they are one and all organically united in a sysem of human knowledge, as members of one whole. . ."[10] The history of philosophy is thus the inherent architectonic of reason and its particular shape of manifestation. All philosophical system advocate the self-development of reason, from which they get their organizing schema, and they are then all united in a single organic whole. However, this organic whole cannot emerge at once. Because of the finitude of human reason, it must undergo a process of historization. Kant says: "It is unfortunate that only after we have spent much time in the collection of materials in somewhat random fashion at the suggestion of an idea lying hidden in our minds, and after we have, indeed, over a long period assemble the materials in a merely technical manner, does it become possible for us to discuss the idea in a clearer light, and to devise a whole architectonically in accordance with the ends of reason."[11]

Kant is of the opinion that it is possible to construct the architectonic of human knowledge only because the history of philosophy, which is now coming to an end, has the same organic form as the final system that it brings to light. In other words, *the structure of the history of philosophy is inherently the same as that of the system of philosophy, although it must be concealed and become distorted in the process of its development*. It shows conclusively that Kant anticipates the Hegelian view as regards the dynamics of the history of philosophy. To say that the development of reason is gradual does not mean that it is continuous. Instead it is characterized by periods of accumulation, contradiction, collapse, and radical innovation. Contradictions are inevitable in the *history* of philosophy, where its single component emerge disconnected and in seeming opposition to one another. Hence, the great controversies in the history of philosophy have their origin in the nature of pure reason. The conflicting principles and schools of thought represent different interests of reason, although they do so in partial, confused and one-sided ways. Then they produce genuine *antinomies*, which eventually lead to the breakdown of the respective systems and call for a new "revolution in the mode of thinking" to resolve them. Since reason, however, is fundamentally coherent, this is an indication that it had not been satisfactorily explained. The breakdown of historical systems may temporarily make philosophy into a "field full of ruins", that is, aggregates of disunited concepts, the victim of sceptics who deny the very possibility of rationality. However, it produces a new "need of reason" to overcome this unstable state through a new philosophical *revolution*, and this process continues as long as the new path of the *Critique*, which systematically brings into harmony the various interests of reason and enables its pure system to emerge in full, has not been found.

Then, the endless conflicts between rationalists and empiricists, sceptics and dogmatists, hedonists and purists, stoics and epicureans, piece meal and systematic philosophers notwithstanding, all are historical members of a single organic whole; they are governed by the architectonic of reason and gradually bring its harmony to light. In this respect, Kant's *Critique* is supposed to open the way not just to another reconciling synthesis, but to the most comprehensive systematization of the ends of reason as these relate to one another in the pure framework of reason itself. To understand this issue more fundamentally, we must now consider the architectonic.

The word *architectonic* suggests a plan or schematic design, such as that is used in constructing buildings. It also suggests a functional relation between the construct and the set of *purposes* it is meant to serve. Kant employs both connotations when he uses the term metaphorically to refer to "the act of constructing systems"[12] in general; but he also makes it clear that in order to supply this metaphor to philosophy, further conditions must be met. In particular, all the parts of the system must be devised in relation to each other, and to their totality. And the system must be united by a central purpose that reflects an intrinsic end or interest of reason.

The key concept of architectonic is thus the essential or intrinsic ends of human reason. However, at first Kant defines the architectonic much more broadly, as "the doctrine of what is scientific in our knowledge",[13] and also, as we have seen, as the art of systematization in general. These two initial definitions are related, since only systematic unity can elevate a body of knowledge to the rank of a science. Hence philosophy, too, must be systematic if it is to quality as scientific. In other words, it cannot be an aggregate of piece meal philosophical discoveries and particular concepts formed here and there, but must — as the current definition of philosophy puts it — become the "*system* of all philosophical knowledge," and give the latter "logical completeness."[14] However, this is only the "scholastic" definition of philosophy, which is not sufficiently informative by ignoring a vital element. Granting that philosophy must be systematic, the problem is to know what *kind* of systematic form is adequate to philosophy. Is "logical completeness" adequate or is it necessary to resort to a higher systematic organization, involving the concept of a purpose?

Kant's answer to this question is the crux of the architectonic. The proper form of philosophy is indeed teleological. The element of purpose spelled out in the ends of reason *belongs to the objective system of philosophy and actually serves to articulate it*. To be properly *systematized*, philosophy must therefore refer all branches of theory to the "essential ends of reason". It cannot be satisfied with discovering the foundations of the various disciplines, both philosophical and non-philosophical, without relating them to their ultimate *ends*; and it must not take these ends from extrinsic sources (like technology, or politics, or theology, or simple intellectual entertainment), but from the very nature of rationality as a self-sufficient interest.

Kant defines philosophy according to its 'world concept'. He says: "...., philosophy is the science of the relation of all knowledge to the essential ends of human reason (*teleologia rationis humanae*), and the philosopher is not an artificer in the field of reason, but himself the law giver of human reason."[15] The architectonic of reason — the supreme ruler of its systematization — requires that all its ingredients be referred to a set of rational *goals* or tasks inhere in the rational attitude itself; and these must be followed for their own sake and eventually become harmonized in relation to the highest good. Positing the highest good as the supreme end of reason that systematizes all the others, introduces the primacy of pure practical reason into the definition of philosophy as wisdom. According to Kant, philosophy is the research of wisdom, and wisdom is the agreement of the will with the final end (the highest good). Given this view, wisdom becomes not a mode of knowledge but a certain *moral* attitude, a mode of the will.

The 'history' has two common uses, one referring to what the historian does (historiography), and one referring to what the historian writes about (substantive history). So far I have discussed the substance of the philosophy, showing its latent architectonic or organic nature. But Kant holds that this nature must also reflect on the field of historiography. He ends the critique with a section, "The History of Pure Reason", outlining a further, still incomplete part of the system. He says: "This title shows here only in order to indicate one remaining division of the system, which future workers must complete. I content myself with casting a cursory glance, form a purely transcendental point of view, namely, that of the nature of pure reason, on the works of those who have laboured in this field — a glance reveals (many stately) structures, but in ruins only."[16]

This programatic passage makes it clear that Kant has in mind a *philosophical* historiography of philosophy, written from a "transcendental", not an empirical point of view. It is made possible by the organic substance of the history of philosophy; and since it would be written from the standpoint "of the nature of pure reason", a philosophical historiography of philosophy would qualify as an integral part of the system of philosophy, and serve together with the Architectonic as its meta-physical theory. This is why Kant insists that a rational history of this kind *must* be added. On the other hand, it comes as the last step, as a compliment that does not require the same innovative revolution necessary for the *Critique* itself. Once the nature of pure reason is completely brought to light, it will provide the paradigm by which one can turn back empirical history, grasp its holistic structure and trace the marks of the architectonic of reason within it.

Kant makes a distinction between a rational and a merely historical historiography of philosophy as follows. A historical (empirical) representation of philosophy tells the story how people have hitherto philosophized, and in what order. But philosophy is a gradual development of human reason, which could not have progressed — nor begun — in the empirical way, be it even though mere concepts. Hence, Kant feels the need for a philosophical history of philosophy is not itself historical or empirical, but rational, that is, *a priori* possible. For even if it, too, puts forth the facts of reason, it does not borrow from them the narration of history, but derives them, as a philosophical archaeology, from the nature of human reason. He further points out that a history of philosophy is of such a special nature, that in it nothing can be told of what *has* happened, without knowing previously what *should* have happened. For it is not the history of opinions that arose here and there, but of reasons that develops itself through concepts. Kant recognizes that *one cannot write a history of things that did not occur*. Therefore, his problem is not to derive the historical states a *priori*, but to identify the developing pattern of reason *within* the diversity of empirical material. The signs of what "should have happened" must be discovered in what did happen, without eliminating the latter, but without accepting it as *merely* contingent. This is why no strict correspondence between the rational schema and the empirical theory of philosophy can be found, although the former must be traceable in the latter. The plan of reason can be known only at the end, and each philosopher is groping after it in indistinct awareness. This gives the philosophical historian of philosophy a clear advantage not only over the empirical historian, but also over the great philosophers of the past: he can understand their systems better than they did themselves.

R.G. Collingwood rightly summarizes Kant's theory of history in four points as follows: "(i) *Universal history* is a feasible ideal, but demands a union of historical and philosphical thought; the facts must be understood as well as narrated, seen from within and not only from outside. (ii) It presupposes a *plan,* i.e., it exhibits a *progress,* or shows something as coming progressively into being. (iii) That which is thus coming into existence is *human rationality,* i.e., intelligence, moral freedom. (iv) The means by which it is being brought into existence is *human irrationality,* i.e., passion, ignorance, selfishness."[17]

Appendix

Prof. J.B. Bhattacharjee is one of the renowned historians of India. In my considered opinion, he is a philosophical historian rather than a mere empirical historian. He points out that "The historical research in North-East has been striving forward towards reconstruction of the past of the societies and communities in the region...."[18] Needless to point out that he advocates a teleological account of history in general and history of North-East in particular. "Striving forward" indicates the *becoming* of history. He talks about the "progressive reorientation"[19] of history. He is of the view that history is a science. In this connection, he is worth quoting in full. He says: "The old notion that history is just a study of the past is doomed to demolition. History is, in effect, a *science* (italics are mine) of study in retrospect; it is a process and continuity. It is not a study of the past for past's sake; its concern is the present and the future of the society. It is not a study of the past that is behind the society; history's past is living and moving in shaping the future."[20] According to him, history is goal-oriented. I am sure that Prof. Bhattacharjee refers to historiography or what the historian does when he talks about "reconstruction of the past." It is worth reiterating that Kant is of the conviction that one cannot write a history of things that did not occur. Prof. Bhattacharjee echoes a corresponding view, if not an identical view, when he says that "... to visualize the future development in a historical perspective, it is necessary that he (the historian) knows the past thoroughly well."[21] These views of Prof. Bhattacharjee come very close to Kant's view on history. In this respect, that is, as a historian, he is a Kantian, and not a Kantian in respect of Kant's epistemology, meta-physics, aesthetics and moral philosophy. This has to be understood very carefully without having any preconceived petty prejudices. Prof. Bhattacharjee broadly agrees with J.D. Barnal, when he says: "In science, more than any other human situation, it is necessary to search out the past in order to understand the present and to control the future."[22] Prof. Bhattacharjee adds to the above quoted passage by saying that "In this process, that 'history repeats itself' can be *scientifically* (italics are mine) established."[23]

Prof. S.K. Bhuyan, another great historian of North-East India, too, comes very close to holding the Kantian position as regards history since he could be reasonably considered to be a Hegelian, at least in principle.[24] Prof. S. K. Bhuyan is a Kantian indirectly since Hegel borrows this concept from Kant.

REFERENCES

1. Immanuel Kant, *Critique of Pure Reason*, A. 835/B.863, p. 655, Norman Kemp Smith (Trans.), Macmillan, London, 1973.
2. Kant says, "By an architectonic I understand the art of constructing systems. As systematic unity is what first raises ordinary knowledge to the rank of science, that is, makes a system out of an aggregate of knowledge; architectonic is the doctrine of the scientific in our knowledge, and therefore necessarily form of the doctrine of method." (*Ibid.*, p. 653).
3. Immanuel Kant, *Foundation of Metaphysics of Morals*, Tr. By L.W. Beak (Chicago, 1950).
4. Immanuel Kant, *Religion Within the Limits of Reason Alone*, Tr. by T.M. Greene and H.H. Hudson, VI: 5/5, (New York, 1960).
5. *Ibid.*, VI: 4/4.

6. Immanuel Kant, *Critique of Practical Reason*, Tr. By L.W. Beck, (New York: 1956), V: 10/115.
7. Immanuel Kant, *Critique of Judgement*, Tr. By J.C. Meredith (Oxford, 1952).
8. Immanuel Kant, *Religion Within the Limits of Reason Alone*, Tr. By T.M. Greene and H.H. Hudson (New York, 1960), VI: 5/5.
9. Immanuel Kant, *Critique of Pure Reason*, *op. cit.*, A. 856/B, 884.
10. *Ibid.*, A., 835/B. 863.
11. *Ibid.*
12. *Ibid.*, A. 832/B.860.
13. *Ibid.*
14. *Ibid.*, A.838/B.866.
15. *Ibid.*, A.839/B.867.
16. *Ibid.*, A.852/B.880.
17. R.G. Colling Wood, *The Idea of History*, Oxford University Press, p. 103.
18. J.B. Bhattacharjee, Presidential Address, *Proceedings of North East India History Association (NEIHA)*, Fourteenth Session, Jorhat, 1993, Kamala Press, Shillong, 1994, p. 1.
19. *Ibid.*, p. 2.
20. *Ibid.*
21. *Ibid.*, p. 9.
22. Quoted by Prof. J.B. Bhattacharjee in his Presidential Address to History, Archaeology and Culture Session, *XVII Indian Social Science Congress*, August 10-15, 1993, R.V. College of Engineering, Bangalore, p. 16.
23. Ibid.
24. S.C. Daniel, "Hegel's Philosophy of History — A Critical Evaluation', *Proceedings of North East India History Association*, Fifteen Session, Doimukh, 1994, Modern Offset, Shillong, pp. 21–22.

CHAPTER 6

Hegel's Philosophy of History—A Critical Evaluation

(George Wilhelm Friedrich Hegel, 1770–1831)

George William Hegel occupies a central place in philosophy in particular, and in the history of thought in general. However, Hegel's philosophy was pushed to the background for a considerable period of time. Students of philosophy have only a perfunctory acquaintance with Hegel's philosophy. They study him, if at all they do, only as a German Idealist who advocates what has come to be known as 'Objective Idealism'. However, it is heartening to note that there has been a renewed interest in Hegel's philosophical thoughts especially in France and Germany. Nevertheless, even this renewed interest manifests itself only in the areas of his metaphysical and religious ideas. And the object of this belated interest has been his phenomenal and monumental work, namely *Phenomenology of the Spirit*, which resulted in an extraordinary revaluation in the light of the Marxist sequel to Hegel's thought. As a result, another important work of his probably his *magnum opus*, *The Philosophy of History*[1] has been neglected, and almost forgotten for a long time. And yet, *The Philosophy of History* remains the heart and centre of Hegel's philosophy. It is no exaggeration to say that this book has had the most profound influence over the years. And rightly so; for Hegel's whole philosophy is historically conceived. Karl Lowith corroborates this view, when he says: "His (Hegel's) whole system is as fundamentally thought out in historical terms as no other philosophy before him.[2] Almost all his basic notions, such as the World Spirit, Reason, Freedom and the like receive their meaning and significance within a historical context. This article makes an endeavour to present an exposition of some of these basic notions. What is an exposition? Kant, one of the greatest philosophers of all times, defines the term exposition as follows: "*By exposition (expositio)* I mean the clear, though not necessarily exhaustive, representative of that which belongs to a concept...."[3] I would try to emulate Kant. This is not to claim that I would be able to emulate Kant completely; for I am a Lilliput and as compared to Gulliver Kant.

Hegel conceives history as the march to Freedom through the world. This march of Freedom is interpreted as what the world Spirit wants while it tries to realize itself. It may be noted here that Hegel was a Lutheran (He was a protestant adhering Martin Luther's doctrine of justification by faith alone), and he had the firm conviction that history consisted in realizing the fullest import of the Christian message, that is, the fullest realization of Universal Spirit. According to Hegel, Freedom consists in a conscious recognition and acceptance of the good, which Christian system of values contains.

The attainment of Rational Freedom is recognized and acknowledged by all optimistic thinkers in history. The goal is the self-realization, the complete development of Spirit, whose intrinsic or essential nature is freedom – freedom in both senses of the term, that is, liberation from *outward* control as well as the emancipation from the *inward* slavery of lust and passion.

Hegel advocates Universal History. There are other sorts of History as well, he points out. These are three in number, namely I. Original History, II. Reflective History, and III. Philosophical History. Those who employ Original History describe the deeds, events, and states of society of their times. They simply transfer what happens in the society around them. They thus internalize the external phenomena. They make available the statements and narratives of other people. Their narratives are not very comprehensive since they make them objects of conceptive faculty. Their aim is nothing more than preserving a sequence of events as truthfully as possible to the benefit of future generation. But their attempts remain narrow because they succeed in getting only a fragmentary glimpse of the great world. The second kind of History, that is, Reflective History, transcends the present. We can distinguish a variety of species in this second order, which are as follows. (1) Historians who adopt this method may be termed as compilers because of the fact that they compile the historical materials. These historians (compilers), instead of writing history become cerebral and try to discover how history ought to be written. They attempt to present individual representations of the past on the basis of mere abstraction, (2) this second species of Reflective History may be categorized as *Pragmatical*. These pragmatical historians bring the past to bear upon the present conditions of things. They try to arrange and manipulate historical materials in their own individualistic ways. Their history falls much short of being holistic, (3) the third species of Reflective History is known as *Critical*. We may even call it a History of History; for it presents a criticism of historical narratives and an investigation of their truth and credibility. It is true that this sort of history tries to present something more than the recorded matters. But it does not stop with a merely critical procedure for substantial history – it also includes the judgements of the historians. Thus most of the historical data are replaced by subjective whims and fancies, and (4) this species of Reflective History takes an abstract position. However, it forms a transition to the Philosophical History of the world since it takes general points of view of History of Art, of Law, and of Religion. III. The third kind of history is characterized as *philosophical*. This sort of history demands an exposition of justification unlike the first two (I and II) mentioned above since their nature is self-evident. Hegel defines philosophy of history as follows: "The most general definition that can be given, is, that the philosophy of History means nothing but the *thoughtful consideration of it*."[4] He is of the considered view that thought is essential to humanity. The task of philosophy, according to him, is as follows. I quote: "The only thought which philosophy brings with it to the contemplative of History, is the simple conception of Reason; that Reason is the sovereign of the world; that the history of the world, therefore, presents us with a rational process."[5] Hegel does not want the philosopher to introduce *a priori* inventions of their own into the records of the past — he exhorts the philosophers to proceed historically — empirically. He opines that to *explain* history is to depict the activities of the human kind.

Hegel investigates Universal History, which belongs to the realm of *Spirit*. Spirit displays itself in its most concrete reality in Universal History. There are three aspects of Spirit, which are as follows. (1) The abstract characteristics of the nature of spirit, (2) what means Spirit use in order to realize its Idea, and (3) the perfect embodiment of Spirit is manifested in the state. (1) The nature of Spirit is the anti-thesis of Matter. The essence of Matter is Gravity while the essence of Spirit is Freedom. Matter has its essence out of itself while Spirit is *self-contained existence*. And this self-contained existence is what is exactly meant by Freedom. Though one cannot exist independently of something external, one can be free when one's own existence depends upon oneself. The self-contained existence of Spirit is nothing but self-consciousness — consciousness of one's own being. In consciousness two things can be distinguished, namely (1) the fact *that I know*, and (2) *what I know*. But in *self* consciousness these two aspects become one; for spirit *knows itself*. Spirit has the ability to make itself *actually* that which it is *potentially*. In its abstract nature, Universal History exhibits Spirit realizing actuality out of its potentiality, (2) the means which Spirit uses lead to the phenomenon of History itself. The means are external and phenomenal, which present themselves in History to our sensibility. The vast aggregations of volitions, interests, passions, and activities constitute the instruments and means of the World. Spirit brings about consciousness, and thus realizing it, and (3) What is the object to be realized by those means? The object is personality itself — human desires — subjectivity generally. Reason attains positive existence by using human knowledge and volition as its material element. Law is the objectivity of Spirit, which is nothing but volition in its true form. Hegel says: "Only that will which obeys laws, is free; for it obeys itself — it is independent and so free."[6] When the subjective will is subsumed under Law, the contradiction between Liberty and Necessity vanishes. The Rational has necessary existence, and thus objective. The State is the Idea of Spirit in the external manifestation of human will and its Freedom.

History advances to something better, more perfect.[7] Spirit in its completeness, is its essential nature, that is, is Freedom. There are many instances in History where the gain of previous culture appears to have been entirely lost. In such cases, a new beginning has to be made in order to restore the original condition. There is an opposition or contradiction between that which is perfect, and that which is imperfect. However, the contradiction is continually annulled and solved.

Universal History shows the development of the consciousness of Freedom on the part of Spirit, and of the consequent realization of that Freedom. This development implies a gradation, that is, a series of increasingly adequate expressions or manifestation of Freedom. And this development leads to a richer and more concrete shape. The absolute aim of Spirit transcends the obligations and the liability to ascription of good or bad motives. On the other hand, these obligations and ascription of good or bad motives apply only to individuality on the basis of its social relation. The very essence of Spirit is activity. It realizes its own potentiality by making itself an object of itself. Spirit transcends immediate, simple and unreflected existence. Hegel is worth quoting here. He states: *the principles of successive phases of Spirit that animate the Nations in a necessitated gradation, are themselves only steps in the development of the one universal Spirit, which through them elevates and completes itself to a self-comprehending totality*.[8] Again, ... *Spirit is immortal; with it there is no past, no future, but an essential now*.[9]

Let me end with a quotation. C.J. Friedrich succintly and aptly describes Hegel's Philosophy of History as follows. I quote: An extended discussion of the influence of Hegel, more especially of his philosophy of History, would amount to a history of most learning and scholarship, excepting the natural sciences, for the last 125 years. To become acquainted with Hegel is therefore to become acquainted with oneself and one's intellectual background. You may reject Hegel in the end, as I do, but you will have gained perspective of knowing why.

In any case, the reading of *The Philosophy of History* is an exciting and at times a strenuous journey.[10]

REFERENCES

1. G.W.F. Hegel, *The Philosophy of History*, Diver Publications, New York, 1956.
2. Karl Lowith. *Von Hegel Zu Nietzsche*, p. 44.
3. Emmanuel Kant, *Critique of Pure Reason*, (Trans.) Norman Kemp Smith, Macmillan, 1973, p. 68.
4. G.W.F. Hegel. *The Philosophy of History*, p. 8.
5. *Ibid.*, p. 9.
6. *Ibid.*, p. 39.
7. I had the audacity to state in the subject of my article that it may also attempt to relate Hegel's philosophy of history to North-East historical situation (North East India History Association, Abstract of Papers — Fifteenth Session — December 6–8, 1994, Arunachal University, Doimukh, p. 18). Then I realized that it was a case of easier said than done. However, after having committed myself rather impetuously, I decided to do something about this. Fortunately, I had an opportunity to read, *'Some Literacy Reminiscences'* by Surya Kumar Bhuyan (Pragjyotish Granthasala, Gauhati, Assam, 1954), courtesy Prof. Imdad Hussain of the Department of History, North-Eastern Hill University, Shillong. Needless to say that I was overjoyed since I could see the possibility of relating one particular view of S.K. Bhuyan to one of the fundamental principles of Hegel's philosophy of history. S.K. Bhuyan was no ordinary historian. R.K. Moorkerji says: *He (S.K. Bhuyan) has illuminated many a dark space in the history of his people, and has helped us to know more about a little known but very important state of India. His work is marked by a high degree of enthusiasm and idealism which alone can make the dry bones of history live and bring before our eyes once again the buried past"* (Foreword, *Some Literary Reminiscences).*
   Hegel is of the conviction that history advances to something better, more perfect. S.K. Bhuyan has the same conviction. He says in the preface of his book that his readers will be interested in the strivings of a *fellow mortal*. I quote: "the strivings of a fellow mortal in the pursuit of his chosen path, and that *kindred spirits will continue their march to reach the Promised Land of which I have but obtained a distinct gleam and vision."* (Italics are mine). I may note here with happiness that a symposium was organized by NEIHA in its XVth Session on the contribution of S.K. Bhuyan to the historical development in North-East India.
8. *Ibid.*, p. 78.
9. *Ibid.*, p. 79.
10. C.J. Friedrich in his Introduction to *The Philosophy of History.*

CHAPTER 7

Karl Marx's Theory of History

(Karl Marx, 1818–1883)

My aim in this chapter is to state and explain Karl Marx's theory of history. At the outset itself, I must acknowledge freely that everything I say in this paper seems to be quite obvious to me. And I feel strongly that whatever that seems to be obvious to me, for that matter to anyone, must be considered seriously. I agree with the thesis that the more elaborate and comprehensive the normative theory is, the more complete and defined the conceptual framework which accompanies it will be. I hold the view that Karl Marx's theory of history is a normative one. I hasten to add that I am not the first philosopher to look at Karl Marx's theory of history from the normative perspective. A number of philosophers have already done this sort of exercise. It would suffice to cite just one example. Jefferey Reiman has contributed significantly in this direction in his important article entitled, 'Moral Philosophy: The Critique of Capitalism and the Problem of Ideology'.[1] In this paper, I would also try to discuss Karl Marx's theory of history *vis-à-vis* the history/historian(s) of North-East India.

It is imperative on my part, I believe, to explicate what exactly I mean by a normative theory. And this I would do succinctly as follows. Norm means standard, model or pattern. In ethics or moral philosophy, norm means a designated standard of average performance of people of a given age, background, and so on. It also means a standard based on the past average performance of a given individual. 'Normative' pertains to a norm especially an assumed one regarded as the standard of correctness in behaviour. It tends or attempts to establish such a norm by the prescription of rules. Theory means a coherent group of general propositions used as explanation for a class of phenomena. It evidently follows from this that by normative theory I mean moral philosophy; for moral philosophy deals with moral norms and moral phenomena. Moral philosophy has a practical purpose. This practical purpose consists in achieving an end, which is conceived as a higher stage of development than the present one. Moral philosophy does not consider moral knowledge as purely theoretical moral phenomena but as a practical knowledge about how we ought to live. The goal of moral philosophy is not that we should simply know what goodness is but that we should become good.

Karl Marx is one of the most influential figures of the twentieth century as far as the social sciences are concerned. Terrell Carver says, "Marx was a highly original and polymathic thinker, unhampered by disciplinary boundaries, whose intellectual influence has been enormous."[2] I am convinced that we can still learn many things from the works of Marx. We can learn not only from his achievements, but also from his mistakes. I would go to the extent of claiming that his mistakes are more instructive than the achievements of most of the thinkers. Marx tries to work out a science of history. He also tries to account for the rise, persistence and decline of societies. Marxism is not mere observation, analysis, and prediction; it is much more than that. It is very interesting and important to note that Marx considers capitalism as a perennial source of unending *exploitation*. The term 'exploitation' strongly suggests moral condemnation. It is no exaggeration to say that he perceives capitalism as a disvalue, pure and simple. The practical nature of Marxism is very much pronounced. And this practical nature of Marxism brings it into contact with moral philosophy. Moral philosophy is the moral study of logic and foundations of moral principles. And these moral principles consist of propositions about what is morally right or wrong to do, and what is morally good or bad to bring about. The phrases right and wrong are generally acknowledged to be associated with human action, and the phrases good and bad are normally linked to outcomes or consequences. Common examples of moral principles are as follows: (i) 'Thou shalt not kill', (ii) 'Do unto others as you would have others do unto you', (iii) 'Avoid injury to others', and (iv) 'Promote human happiness', 'What is it that makes the above principles moral?'—This is a very fundamental question, no doubt. It is also true that it is an important task of moral philosophers to answer such a basic question. However, I will not try to answer this question for the simple reason that it lies outside the scope of this paper. I shall limit my task only to linking moral philosophy with Marxism. Appeals to morality are different from appeals to self-interests. Moral principles must be *disinterested*, or they must be based on *disinterestedness*, that is, they must be based on reasons other than simply to serve some particular interests, self-interests or interests of other people. I have reasons to believe that Marx recognizes morality as a powerful motivator, guiding people to put aside or even sacrifice their own self-interests to uphold what is right.

Prior to an evaluation of a Marxian moral critique of capitalism, we must determine whether the critique is rightly understood as moral. In order to do this, we must ask whether Marxism entails a normative critique, and if it does, we must ask whether the norm appealed to is a distinctively moral one. This question is answered negatively by those who are convinced that Marxism is nothing but a science of history that attempts to predict the necessary and inevitable collapse of capitalism. They also claim that eventually capitalism will be replaced by communism, of course, via socialism. If this is what Marxism is all about, then norms, whether moral or non-moral, are irrelevant, and the presence of moral norms in Marx's writings must be dismissed as mere accidental. This sort of interpretation has textual evidence. For instance, Marx and Engels proclaim, "The communists do not preach morality at all."[3] They also criticize their contemporary socialists, who recommend socialism on the basis of its moral superiority to capitalism. They called such socialists utopians, and distinguished their position from their own, which they called *scientific,* because it tried to show the inevitability and necessity of socialism as the consequence of the inherent contradictions of capitalism.[4] However, this is not a very satisfactory exposition of Marxism for the following reasons. If the replacement of capitalism by communism is a *necessary event,* then, there is no need for human participation in the struggle, for the outcome is *inevitable* any way. It must be pointed out here that Marx himself felt the urge to participate in political activity in order to alleviate the sufferings of the working class. Marx, therefore, must have known that after all things were not as inevitable as the above mentioned exposition would suggest. Marx was the first Marxist to engage in political activism. Many a Marxist subsequently followed the example set by Marx. Nowadays, political activism is perceived as a natural extension of theoretical views held by the communists. Such practical activity would make sense if and only if the replacement of capitalism by socialism is based on human actions at least to a certain extent. This means that human beings do have choices to choose from. Moreover, if there are norms, the human actions can be decided as to whether they are appropriate or not, against such norms to overthrow capitalism in order to establish communism. It seems justifiable then to claim that since Marxism is as much an invitation to practice as to understanding, it must appeal to some norm or some value capable of justifying that practice. This norm must be a moral norm. 'What moral norm does Marxism appeal?' — This is a very significant question, which needs to be addressed to with utmost care and earnestness. Some Marxists hold the view that Marxism does embrace a norm, *but it is not a moral norm or ideal.* For example, Allen Wood opines that Marx saw nothing morally wrong with capitalism. According to him, Marx condemned capitalism not because it would give rise to moral evils, but because it would give rise to non-moral evils such as crippling human creativity, promoting alienation, encouraging servitude, and so on.[5] This is a questionable view for a very important reason, which is as follows. People disapprove of these evils, and fight against them collectively, often risking their own lives to get rid of them for the welfare of others. If it is the case, it is not at all clear why there are not moral evils and their corrective moral goods.

G.A. Cohen is one of the best known among contemporary Marxist philosophers to defend the view that Marxism condemns capitalism as unjust.[6] Cohen argues that injustice is the proper ground for Marxian condemnation of capitalism. Needless to point out that *justice* and *injustice* alike are moral norms. Though Marx's moral theory is rather fragmentary. Marx's theory of history could be seen as a normative theory. Given this view, one could claim that according to Marx, capitalism is *unjust* while communism is *just*. This clearly shows that Marx takes justice to be the moral norm against which both capitalism and communism ought to be judged.

Moral discourse is not primarily — though sometimes it may be incidentally — informative; but nor is it essentially — though sometimes it may be incidentally — 'emotive'. It does not serve essentially, though it may do consequently, to *influence* people, to get them to do things or refrain from doing them; it is, rather, *action-guiding*. In saying to you, for example, 'you ought to repay the money' I am not, indeed, merely stating some fact; but nor am I, primarily or necessarily, seeking to get you to do something; I am, essentially, telling you *what do to*. A great advantage of considering moral discourse as action-guiding is that it escapes the conclusion that such a discourse is non-rational for the following reason. If moral discourse is action-guiding, it is essential that you should understand what I tell you; you may ask me for my reasons, and consider whether the reasons I give you are good or bad; my answer to your question may be the right answer even if you do not accept it, or wrong even though you accept it without hesitation. To ask for and to give answers to practical questions is plainly and essentially a business for rational beings, and one that can be appraised on rational grounds.

I would like to view Marx's theory of history as a normative theory, which is essentially *action-guiding*. Marx seems to prescribe the moral principles, 'you ought to establish communism', and 'you ought to overthrow capitalism'. Needless to say that these moral principles are based on the moral norm of injustice, that is, 'capitalism is unjust' because it necessarily leads to moral evil, and 'communism' is just because it would bring about the welfare of the working class or proletariat. Marx is engaged in the task of telling us, goading us *what to do* to achieve the desired end. And this action-guiding moral principle is firmly and surely based on rational grounds, that is, reasons are offered in defence of it.

If Marx's theory of history is understood primarily as a normative theory as outlined above, I am sure, it will be able to steer clear of many criticism levelled against it. Consider some of Karl Popper's criticisms of Marx's theory of history. Popper takes Marx's theory of history as a sort of historicism. Now, historicism may mean one of the following three things, namely, (i) the belief that processes are at work in history that man can do little to alter, (ii) the theory that historian must avoid all *value judgements* in his study of past records or former cultures, and (iii) veneration of the past or of tradition. Popper takes historicism to mean (i), that is, the belief that processes are at work in history that man can do little to alter, for he claims to have repudiated historicism by saying that he has succeeded in showing that, for strictly logical reasons, it is impossible for us to predict the future course of history. This is what he says: "I mean by *'historical prediction* is their principal aim, and which assumes that this aim is attainable by discovering the 'rhythms' or the 'patterns', the 'laws' or the 'trends' that underlie the evolution of history... I am convinced that such historist doctrines of method at bottom responsible for the unsatisfactory state of the theoretical social sciences (other than economic theory).[7] Continuing in this vein Popper claims: "My intention is to criticize the doctrine that it is the task of the social sciences to propound historical prophecies, and that historical prophecies are needed if we wish to conduct politics in a rational way. I shall call this doctrine 'historicism'. I consider historicism to be the relic or an ancient superstition, even though the people in it are usually convinced that it is a very new, progressive, revolutionary and scientific theory."[8] It is obvious here that Popper questions the predictive power of history. He also questions the very credentials of history to be considered as 'a very new, progressive, revolutionary and *scientific theory*' (italics are mine). This sort of criticisms is equally applicable to Karl Marx's theory of history, if it is claimed to be a scientific theory or a science of history. But, if we consider Marx's theory of history as a comprehensive normative theory, this criticism becomes vacuous, and it will be an instance of barking at the wrong tree. Another criticism against Marx's theory of history is that it ends up *as a doctrine of determinism* (again, the italics are mine). This attack would become rather misplaced, when Marx's theory is viewed as a normative theory. This sort of criticism is levelled against Marx by many philosophers, especially Popper. He, in his book, *The Open Society and Its Enemies*,[9] considers Plato, Hegel and Marx as enemies of open society since all these three philosophers, according to him, advocate *determinism*.

There is still sufficient disagreement among philosophers as to the exact nature and function of Marx's moral philosophy. Kamenka[10] considers Marx's moral philosophy leads to, what he calls, a sociology of morals. He is worth quoting here. He says: "It was he (Marx) who pointed the way to a sociology of morals, to the recognition of moral codes and moral principles as social demands."[11] On the other hand, Reiman considers Marxism as a special kind of moral philosophy. He says: "... moral philosophy cannot establish the moral credential of any putative moral principle without adequately defending it against the suspicion that it is ideology. Marxism then forces itself onto the agenda of moral philosophy."[12] It may be reiterated here that I have interpreted Marx's theory of history as a kind of moral philosophy, which tries to guide the action of human beings to achieve its highest moral norm or standard or *somun bonum*.

To conclude, Marxist method has been applied in understanding history of North-East. But, it has not been understood from the normative standpoint. I have been arguing in this paper that Marxist method could be considered as a normative one. Though many scholars and historians have employed the Marxist model in understanding the history of the North-East, for some reason or other they have not emphasized the normative aspect of it.

The North-Eastern society presents a very strange situation in that it is multi-ethnic, multi-cultural, multi-linguistic and multi-religious. One of the effective approaches of understanding this pluralism is to apply Marxist model with emphasis on its normative aspect.

REFERENCES

1. Reiman, Jeffrey, "Moral Philosophy: The Critique of Capitalism and the Problem of Ideology" in *The Cambridge Companion to Marx* (ed.) Carver Terrell, Cambridge University Press, 1992, pp. 143-167.
2. Terrell Carver, *The Cambridge Companion to Marx* (ed.) Cambridge University Press, 1992.
3. Marx, Karl, Engels, Frederick. *Collected Works*, New York and London: International Publishers, 1973, p.247.
4. Engels, Frederick. "Socialism, Utopian and Scientific" in *Selected Writings*, (ed.) W.O. Henderson, Harmondsworth: Penguin Books, 1967, pp. 185–225.
5. Wood, Allen, Karl Marx, London, Routledge and Kegan Paul, 1981, p. 43, and "The Marxian Critique of Justice", *Philosophy and Public Affairs*, 1972, 1:224–42, and also "Marx on Right and Justice", *Philosophy and Public Affairs*, 8:267–95.
6. Cohen, G.A. *Karl Marx's Theory of History: A Defense*. Princeton, NJ: Princeton University Press, 1978.
7. Popper, K.R. *The Poverty of Historicism*, Routledge and Kegan Paul, London, 1972, p. 3.
8. Popper, K.R. *Conjectures and Refutations, The Growth of Scientific Knowledge*, Routledge and Kegan Paul, London, 1972, p. 336.
9. Popper, K.R. *The Open Society and Its Enemies*, Routledge and Kegan Paul, London, 1966.
10. Kamenka, E. *Marxism and Ethics*, Macmillan, St. Martin's Press, New York, 1969.
11. *Ibid.*, p. 67.
12. Reiman, Jeffrey. *Op.cit.*, pp. 165–166.

CHAPTER 8

Sri Aurobindo's Theory of History: A Philosophical Investigation

(Sri Aurobindo Ghosh, 1872–1950)

This chapter makes an attempt to show that Sri Aurobindo has a full-blooded theory of history, and that it is a combination of Hegelian Idealism, Indian Idealism and Universalism, especially with regard to religion. This paper will consist of three parts. First part gives an exposition of Sri Aurobindo's theory of history, the second part consists of the attempt to relate his theory to that of Hegelian and Indian Idealism, and the third part tries to show that Sri Aurobindo advocates a much pronounced universal religion, which is different from universal religion as commonly understood.

PART I

The exposition runs as follows. History does not help us to understand humanity because of the fact that it only gives the general story of the past, and the survival of the communities under external conditions. Sri Aurobindo comes down very hard on history. He is worth quoting here. He says: "History teaches us nothing; it is a confused torrent of events and personalities or a Kaleidoscope of changing institution."[1] However, it does not mean that he does not take into account the merits and validity of history. He is only pointing out that it only records swiftly changing scenes by emphasizing the parts rather than the whole. He is also of the view that history is primarily the story of collective ego to the neglect of the individual ego. He opines that history helps us only to understand current or recurrent phenomena, facile generalizations and partial ideas. History is based on incomplete knowledge. He is convinced that social unity can be achieved neither by social nor by political nor by historical devices. The history of past humanity, he avers, reveals that there have been interesting episodes of human life wherein human life has been most efficaciously lived leaving behind many an interesting and illuminating lesson. It was during that time humanity was able to organize itself in little independent centres interacting closely with each other but not joined together with a single unity. India was most productive with lasting results when she comprised of many small kingdoms. Some of them were not bigger than a modern district. The second best followed later on, which comprised of larger but still relatively small nations and kingdoms such as the *Pallavas, Chalukyas, Pandyas, Cholas* and *Cheras*. But India received little from the greater empires that rose and fell within her borders, the *Moghul*, the *Gupta* or the *Maurya*. India gained little in everything except a little in political and administrative organizations, some fine art and literature and a certain amount of lasting work in other kinds, not always of the best quality. Their impulse was rather towards elaborate organization rather than original, stimulating and creative.

Nevertheless, there was always a defect in the regime of small city states or of regional cultures, which necessitated a tendency towards larger organization. This defect invariably led to impermanence, disorder, defenselessness against the attack of much larger organizations, and to a great extent decrease in material well-being. Therefore, this earlier form of collective life tended to disappear resulting in the appearance of nations, kingdoms and empires. The following two things are worth mentioning: (1) the smaller states had the most intense life as compared to the large states and very big empires, and (2) bigger nations and kingdoms were somehow able to generate the most vigorous life by a sort of artificial concentration of the vitality into some centre or capital, London, Paris or Rome. As a consequence, the energy of the district, provincial town and the village was lost irrepairably to a great extent making them dull, petty and drowsy. The individual lost his importance as he was overpowered and overshadowed. It led to staggering stagnation resulting in the stunted growth and suffocation of life itself.

The entire process of Nature depends on a balancing and a continuous tendency to harmonize two opposite ends of life, namely the individual who is nourished by the whole or aggregate and the whole or aggregate which is constituted by the individual. The perfection of human life consists in the harmony between these two different principles of our very own existence, the individual and the social aggregate. History had a very important role to play here. It has preserved for us discrete instances of this anguish or pain, that is, episodes of failure and success. It must be noted here that these instances of travail are enormously instructive for the humanity. The progress towards harmony is strewn with many a difficulty, especially a strife of force. So much so that sometimes it seems to move not towards concord or mutual agreement but towards mutual annihilation. And this annihilation is not of one by the other but of each by the other, so that both shall live entirely in the other and as the other, in the highest ideal of oneness. Paradoxically, strife leads to an increasing mutual understanding, which makes real oneness possible. Strife makes a compromise between two conflicting egoisms. However, it does not fuse these two conflicting things into each other. There is a tension between two equally strong human tendencies, namely individualism and collectivism, that is, between distinctive freedom, perfection and development of the individual being and the powerful authority, perfection and development of the state.

If we consult only the available facts of history, we are forced to hypothesize that our race began with the all-absorbing group to which the individual was entirely secondary, and that increasing individuality is a consequence of human growth, a result of increasing conscious Mind. However, there is also the ancient tradition of humanity according to which the social state was preceded by another, free and unsocial. The tradition is rather that of a golden age in which the individual was freely social without society. He was not restrained by laws or institution; he lived by natural instinct or free knowledge. He neither preyed on his fellow beings nor was he restrained by the burden of the collectivity. It is quite possible that our progress has not been in straight line, but in cycles. In those cycles there have been periods of partial realization. And this partial realization enabled men to live according to the high dream of 'philosophic anarchism'. Philosophic Anarchism means the theory that all forms of government are incompatible with individual social liberty and that such governments should be abolished. During this philosophic Anarchism people lived by inner law of love, and they had right thinking leading to right action; they were not forced to have unity by kings and parliaments, laws and policings and punishments due to petty or great oppression and repression and ugly selfishness and corruption which accompany the forced government of man by man. It is even possible that our original state was an instinctive animal spontaneity of 'free and fluid association'. As a result, the ultimate ideal state will be an enlightened, intuitive spontaneity of 'forces and fluid association'. Our final destiny may be that the original animal association may lead to a community of gods. Sri Aurobindo says, "our progress may be a devious round leading from the easy and spontaneous uniformity and harmony which reflects Nature to the self-possessed unity which reflects the Divine."[2]

History tells us of man as an individual in the more or less organized group. And, there are always two types in the group; one asserts the state idea at the cost of the individual, another asserts the supremacy of state with certain concessions to the individual. A third type has come into existence besides the two mentioned above. And this type is willing to give as much as possible to the individuals; it openly asserts that it exists for his growth assuring his freedom, dignity and development. It has become almost an article of faith according to which this type will bring about the well-being, strength and expansion of the state. England entertained such a faith for a period of time, whatever may be the nature of the state, it cannot be denied that the state tries to wantonly subordinate to itself the free will, the free action, the power and self-assertion of the individuals constituting it. It is palpably false that state is something greater than the individuals constituting it. The State claims without any right that it has the rightful but oppressive supremacy over individual.

In modern times, the State idea has reasserted itself and has been dominating the thought action of the world. Its support is based on two motives, namely (i) it appeals to the external interests of the race, and (ii) it appeals to its moral tendencies. It claims that man shall live for the whole, the group, the community without living for himself. It asserts that the hope and progress of humanity lies in the efficiency and organization of the state. The state tries to have 'mobilization' of the intellect, capacity, thought, emotion, life of the individual, in fact, of all that he is and has, by the state in the interests of all.

Theoretically, it is the subordination of the individual to the good of all that is demanded; practically, it is his subordination to a collective egoism, which tries to satisfy its aims and ambitions by imposing them on the great majority of individuals by a smaller or larger group of persons, who are supposed to represent the community. There is no guarantee whatsoever that the ruling class represents the best mind of the nation. Modern politician does not represent the soul of a people or its aspirations. He represents only the average pettiness, selfishness, egoism and self-deception. However, Nature does move forward in the midst of all shortcomings. Theoretically, collective wisdom stands for the general good. Practically, it does not happen. In fact, it is the energy of the individual which is really efficacious for collective progress.

The organized state is neither the best mind of the nation nor is it even the sum of the communal energies. The collective egoism is far inferior to the best of which the community is capable. The individual has usually something at least like a soul, and he is able to make up for the deficiencies of the soul by means of a system of morality, fear of social opinion, fear of communal laws, and so on, while the State idea lacks such external checks. The State has no soul or has only a rudimentary one. 'A sacred egoism' is still the idea of nations. The State is a convenience, rather a clumsy convenience for our common development; it ought never to be made an end in itself.

The State is not an organism; it is a machinery, and it works like a machine, without fact, taste, delicacy or intuition. It tries to manufacture, but what humanity is here to do is to grow and create. The State tends always to uniformity, but uniformity is death, not life. A State education, a State religion, a State culture are unnatural violences.

A healthy unity of mankind cannot be brought about by machinery. Sri Aurobindo explicates the ideal unification of mankind as follows. He says, "In principle, ... the ideal unification of mankind would be a system in which, as a first rule of common and harmonious life, the human peoples would be allowed to form their own groupings according to their national divisions of locality, race, culture, economic convenience and not according to the more violent accidents of history or the egoistic will of powerful nations whose policy it must always be to compel the smaller or less timely organized to serve their interests as dependents or obey their commands as subjects."[3] The first principle of human unity should be a system of free and natural groupings which would leave no room for internal discord, incompatabilities, repression and revolt as between race and race, or people and people.

It is possible to construct a precarious and quite mechanical unity by political and administrative means. But it can never become a real unity unless the unity is brought about by the religion of humanity; for the religion of humanity spiritualizes itself and becomes the general inner law of human life. Nature drives mankind towards international unification by means of war or conquest, or the temporary dominations of the power State or empire or menance of such a domination which will compel those threatened to adopt a closer system of union. There is also a common uniting sentiments among the individuals. And this sentiment may work in two ways, namely (1) it may come before as an originating or contributory cause, and (2) it may come afterwards as a cementing result.

A spiritual religion of humanity is the hope of the future. This spiritual religion is not what is commonly called a universal religion, a system, a thing of creed and intellectual belief and dogma and outward rite. The religion of humanity means the growing realization that there is a secret spirit, a divine Reality, in which we are all one, that humanity is its highest present vehicle on earth, that the human race and human being are the means by which it will progressively reveal itself here. It shall bring about the 'Kingdom of divine Spirit on earth'. There must be a realization by the individual that only in the life of his fellowmen is his own life complete. There must be realization by the race that only on the free and full life of the individual can its own perfection and permanent happiness be founded. Each man develops within himself a discipline and a way of salvation in accordance with this religion so that it may be developed in the life of the race. The truth of the spirit may step in and lead humanity to the path of its highest possible happiness and perfection. All mechanical solutions are temporary and disappointing.

PART II

One of the most important works of Hegel, probably the most important work is *The Philosophy of History*. This book brings out the best of Hegel's philosophy. And it has been influencing the philosophers and the historians alike greatly since its publication. It should be pointed out that Hegel's philosophy is historically conceived. His whole system of philosophy has been thought out in historical terms. His basic notions such as World Spirit, Reasons and Freedom derive their significance within a historical context. Hegel propounds Universal History. He contends that philosophy of history is nothing but the thoughtful consideration of history. The business of Philosophy, according to him, is to view the history of the world as a rational process since Reason is the 'sovereign' of the world. He also opines that history depicts and explains the activities of the human kind. Universal History belongs to realm of Spirit because Spirit displays itself in its most concrete reality. Reason attains positive existence by using human knowledge and volition as its material element. Law is the objectivity of spirit, which is nothing but volition in its true form. Hegel believes that history advances to something better, more perfect. The very existence of spirit is activity. Spirit transcends immediate, simple and unreflected existence.

It must be noted here that Sri Aurobindo does not consider Reason to be the sovereign of the world because he talks about the end of the Age of Reason to make way for a deeper spirit. Sri Aurobindo and Hegel, advocate idealistic theories for the following reason. Both affirm that mind or spiritual is of central importance in reality. Both also regard reality as essentially spiritual or the embodiment of mind or reason. Though Sri Aurobindo and Hegel advocate idealistic theories, they differ fundamentally in certain respect. For Hegel, Reason is the sovereign of the world. But for Sri Aurobindo, it is not Reason, but something that is suprarational is supreme. Suprarational means that which transcends the rational, and that which cannot be comprehended by reason alone. Hegel gives primacy to Spirit while Sri Aurobindo gives primacy to Nature. Hegel advocates only western idealism while Sri Aurobindo advocates both western and Indian Idealism. Indian Idealism conceives reality as spiritual in nature; it explains everything else as existing in and through it. Indian Idealism believes in unity in diversity or diversity in oneness. It is no exaggeration to say that Sri Aurobindo emphasizes the idea of human unity.

PART III

Sri Aurobindo advocates a spiritual religion of humanity, which is akin to universal religion. But this universal religion is different from what is ordinarily meant by Universal religion. And this universal religion may be called as universal religion so called in order to distinguish it from Sri Aurobindo's spiritual religion or genuine universal religion. Genuine universal religion believes that we are one, and that it makes the life complete while the universal religion so called is based on a system, creed, intellectual belief and dogma. It must be noted that the genuine universal religion is based on intuition, not on stumbling human reason. Sri Aurobindo is a true universalist as far as the religion of humanity is concerned. There are mainly two theories of religion, and the two theories are: (1) Particularism, and (2) Universalism.

Particularism holds that experience is the source of knowledge. Particularism with regard to religion leads to pluralism of religion. This is borne out by the fact that there is a multiplicity of religion. So much so that it is difficult even to list all the existing religions. There has been a conflict between believers of various religious systems. This conflict has been dividing humanity for the past many centuries. Universalism leads to genuine Universal religion. Genuine universal religion claims that there is only one religion, that is, the religion of humanity. Sri Aurobindo is convinced that this sort of religion is the only hope of humanity to end the strife, tension and war between man and man, between race and race, and between nation and nation.

As it has been pointed above Sri Aurobindo advocates Hegelian Idealism. Same thing can be said of S.K. Bhuyan since he is also an upholder of Hegelian Idealism. After having read his book, *Some Literacy Reminiscences*,[4] I am convinced that it is possible to relate one particular view of S.K. Bhuyan to one of the fundamental principles of Hegel's philosophy of history. S.K. Bhuyan was a historian of great importance *vis-a-vis* the history of North-East India. R.C. Moorkerji, another great historian of India, has the following to say about S.K. Bhuyan. He says: "He (S.K. Bhuyan) has illuminated many a dark space in the history of his people, and has helped us to know more about a little known but very important state of India (Assam). His work is marked by a high degree of enthusiasm and idealism which alone can make the dry bones of history live and bring before our eyes once again the buried past."[5]

Needless to point out that Hegel is of the firm conviction that history advances to something better, more perfect. It must be pointed out that S.K. Bhuyan has the same conviction. He says in the preface of his above mentioned book that his readers will be interested in the strivings of a *fellow mortal* — this brings out the great humility of a great historian. I quote: "... in the strivings of a fellow mortal in the pursuit of his chosen path, and that *kindred spirits will continue their march to reach the Promised Land of which I have but obtained a distinct gleam and vision.*"[6] (Italics are mine).

I have endeavoured to show in this paper that Sri Aurobindo advocates a kind of universal religion, which is fundamentally different from the notion of universal religion that is commonly prevalent. Though it is not possible to find a parallel to Sri Aurobindo's kind of universal religion, it is possible to find some semblance of it in the history of the North-East India. It is only a semblance, an indication towards the formation of a spiritual religion of humanity. N.N. Bhattacharyya, in his book, *Religious Culture of North-Eastern India*,[7] tries to connect all the goddesses of North-Eastern India with that of mother goddess Kamakhya of Assam.[8] He also tries to connect all the goddesses of North-Eastern India with the great process of Sanskritization. He underlines the Trantic culture *vis-à-vis* the goddesses of North-East region. This kind of relatedness and connectedness may be taken as a move towards the realization of Sri Aurobindo's kind of universal religion.

REFERENCES

1. Sri Aurobindo, Social and Political Thought, Vol.15, Sri Aurobindo Ashram, Pondicherry, 1971, p. 261.
2. *Ibid.*, p. 274.
3. *Ibid.*, p. 406.
4. Surya Kumar Bhuyan, *Some Literary Reminiscences*, Pragjyotish Granthasala, Gauhati, Assam, 1954.
5. *Ibid.*, R.K. Moorkerji, Foreword.
6. *Ibid.*, S.K. Bhuyan, Preface.
7. N. N. Bhattacharyya, *Religious Culture of North-Eastern India*, Manchar, 1995.
8. *Ibid.*, Chapter III.

CHAPTER 9

Karl Popper and the Poverty of Historicism — A Critical Study

(Karl Raimand Popper, 1902–1996)

Let me begin with a truism. Historiography and historicism are intimately related, if not necessarily connected. Historiography may be defined as principles of methodology of historical study or as the writing of history or as the historical literature. However, historiographers of modern times consider historiography primarily as principles of methodology of historical study.; In my considered opinion, however, the task of historiography is to maintain and preserve the continuity of the past into the present. Historicism may mean one of the following three things, namely (i) the belief that processes are at work in history that man can do little to alter, (ii) the theory that historian *must* avoid all *value judgements* in his study of past records or former cultures, and (iii) veneration of the past or of tradition.

Popper takes the term historicism to mean (i), for he claims to have repudiated historicism by saying that he has succeeded in showing that, for strictly logical reasons, it is impossible for us to predict the future course of history. This is what he says:

"I mean by 'historicism' an approach to the social sciences which assumes that *historical prediction* is their principal aim, and which assumes that this aim is attainable by discovering the 'rhythms' or the 'patterns', the 'laws' or the 'trends' that underlie the evolution of history .... I am convinced that such historicist doctrines of method at bottom responsible for the unsatisfactory state of the theoretical social sciences other than economic theory."[1] Continuing in this vein Popper claims: "My intention is to criticize the doctrine that it is the task of the social sciences to propound historical prophecies, and that historical prophecies are needed if we wish to conduct politics in a rational way. I shall call this doctrine 'historicism'. I consider historicism to be the relic of an ancient superstition, even though the people who believe in it are usually convinced that it is a very new, progressive, revolutionary and scientific theory."[2]

Popper points out that his argument for the refutation of historicism may be summed up in five statements which are as follows:

(1) The course of human history is strongly influenced by the growth of human knowledge. (The truth of this premise must be admitted even by those who see in our ideas, including our scientific ideas, merely the by-products of *material* developments of some kind or other).
(2) We cannot predict, by rational or scientific methods, the future growth of our scientific knowledge.
(3) We cannot, therefore, predict the future course of human history.
(4) This means that we must reject the possibility of a *theoretical history*; that is to say, of a historical social science that would correspond to *theoretical physics*. There can be no scientific theory of historical development serving as a basis for historical prediction.
(5) The fundamental aim of historicist methods is therefore misconceived; and historicism collapses.[3]

The decisive step in this argument, Popper claims, is statement (2). He elaborates this statement as follows:

... *if there is much a thing as growing human knowledge, then we cannot anticipate today what we shall know only tomorrow.*[4] (italics are original). This paper makes an attempt to refute this statement. The logical method adopted to reject the whole argument is as follows. The conclusion of this argument is a conjunction of four conjuncts. If one of the conjuncts is proved to be false, the whole argument collapses. I would, therefore, try to falsify the conjunct (2).

I am well aware of the fact of what I am getting into. I am trying to invalidate an argument, which has been advanced by one of the most influential philosophers of science. He has a great reputation, which extends far beyond the realm of academic philosophy. His ideas on historicism are original and most thought provoking. However, after having had the temerity to cross swords with great Popper, I have decided to go ahead, and tread the path which most of the philosophers fear to tread.

Before I take up the decisive step in the argument of Popper, I would like to outline some of the central ideas of him albeit briefly, in order to examine his views about historicism carefully. Popper holds that "social entities such as institutions or associations" are "abstract models constructed to interpret certain selected abstract relations between individuals."[5] If this theory means that in the social world only individuals are observable, but not social phenomena, it is palpably false for the simple reason that some social phenomena such as weddings and parliamentary procedures can be observed like any natural phenomenon such as trees and forests. However, it may be noted here that both individual and social phenomena have observable as well as non-observable features. If the theory means that individuals exist independently of social groups and institutions, this is also false, since, just as facts about social phenomena are contingent upon fact about individuals, the reverse is also true. Thus, we can only speak of soldiers because we can speak of armies and *vice-versa*. If the theory means that all social phenomena are fictional and all individual phenomena are factual, that would entail that all assertions about social phenomena are false or else neither true nor false, which is absurd. Finally, the theory may be taken to mean that only facts about individuals are explanatory. And if it is taken this way, it will lead to methodological individualism. I may quote here Watkin's account of 'the principle of methodological of individualism'.[6]

According to this principle, the ultimate constituents of the social world are people who act more or less appropriately in the light of their dispositions and understanding of their situation. Every complex social situation or event is the result of a particular configuration of individuals, their dispositions, situations, beliefs, and physical resources and environment. Popper advocates a similar view. This is what he says:

"... all social phenomena, and especially the functioning of all social institutions, should always be understood as resulting from the decisions, actions, attitudes etc. of human individuals, and we should never be satisfied by an explanation in terms of so-called 'collectives'..."[7]

This theory as held by Popper is open to a very serious criticism, which consists in the fact that it can be refuted by a single counter-instance. And this theory contains within itself a dogma of the form 'x is impossible', which can be easily overturned by a single counter-instance. Since such counter-instances are readily available there is nothing more to say on this score. It is ironical that Popper himself provides some.[8] It will suffice to cite one such example: "You cannot have full employment without inflation."[9]

However, I agree with Popper that any attempt to promote a social science the pattern of the nature of the natural sciences is bound to fail. I have pointed this out elsewhere.[10] I also agree with him that determinism and social sciences cannot go together. Given these views, it becomes obvious that 'complete' prediction of the future in social sciences can be ruled out without much ado. A particular distinction made by Popper is worth considering here. The much talked about distinction is as follows. The prediction based on causal laws is basically or fundamentally different from the prediction based on extrapolating trends.[11] The former is based on causal laws while the latter is not. It may be noted here that according to Popper, the predictions in social sciences especially in History are based on the latter. It evidently follows from this that predictions in History are extremely tentative and short-range, and not definitive and long-range. However, it does not mean that long-range predictions or forecasts are not possible in social sciences. As a matter of fact, these sorts of predictions are made by social scientists.

Burke in his book, *The Philosophy of Popper*[12] sets out Popper's general 'refutation of historicism' as follows. Popper's refutation turns on the theoretical impossibility of predicting our responses to future situations. Popper's argument goes as follows. Social and political developments are strongly influenced by scientific developments. This means that our responses to practical problems are determined to a great extent by our earlier responses to theoretical ones. Thus the growth of knowledge is a major influence on the course of human history. But 'we cannot predict, by rational or scientific methods, the future growth of our scientific knowledge' and hence we cannot predict the future course of history. Thus we cannot have a theoretical history, or theoretical social science like that of theoretical physics and astronomy. Hence it is in principle impossible to carry out the historicist programme successfully.

The decisive step in the argument, as Popper says, is the assertion that, if there is such a thing as the growth of human knowledge, then 'we cannot anticipate today what we shall only know tomorrow'.

Burke points out that Popper's italicized principle, that 'we cannot anticipate today what we shall only know tomorrow' is either tautologous or false. Tautologous means needless repetition in the same sense in different words, or redundancy. If by 'anticipating' knowledge we mean actually possessing it, then the said principle is tautologous in the following two different ways: (i) If we can anticipate or possess knowledge today, it is needless to say that we can anticipate or possess knowledge tomorrow, and (ii) if we cannot anticipate or possess knowledge today, it is needless to say that we cannot anticipate or possess knowledge tomorrow. Again, Burke opines that the said principle is false for the following reason. If we take 'scientific means of predicting' to mean predicting the actual results, it would simply be a case of speeding up present research. I would, therefore, be nonsense to call it a means of *prediction* at all.

Though I admire and owe much to Burke's illuminating and penetrating analysis of Popper's italicized principle, I would like to tackle the same in my own way. It is worth reiterating that this italicized principle is the explanation of premise No. 2. Before I criticize this premise, I would like to have a careful look at the premise No. 1. This premise states 'the course of human history is strongly influenced by the growth of human knowledge'. Popper identifies the growth of human knowledge with the growth of our ideas including scientific ideas and the by-products of material developments of all kinds. This he says in the parenthesis of premise No. 1, which I quote in full.

"The truth of this must be admitted even by those who see in our ideas, including our scientific ideas, merely the by-products of *material* developments of some kind or other".[13]

Later on in the premise No. 2, Popper identifies the growth of human knowledge with the future growth of our scientific knowledge. This means that he consistently conflates human knowledge with that of scientific knowledge. This conflation is mistaken because of the fact that human knowledge as such or *per se*, is different from scientific knowledge. Human knowledge as such is constant, which consists in having the ability to use forms, categories and concepts. This remains the same at all times and all places. And it remains the same while what is presented to the human kind varies and it varies tremendously. In the transcendental language, the *Form* remains the same while *matter* or *content* changes. And this is to say that human kind use the *Form* in the same way to interpret the *content* that they receive.[14] This means that though there is a tremendous amount of growth as regards the *content*, the capacity to use the *form* remains unaltered. In other words, the *content* is given to the human kind while the *form* is not given but it is constitutive of human kind. In this connection, I would like to quote A.N. Whitehead, one of the greatest mathematicians of our times. This is what he says:

"The reason why we are on a higher imagination level, is not because we have finer imagination, but because we have better instruments. In science, the most important thing that has happened during the last forty years is the advance in instrumental design. This advance is partly due to a few men of genius such as Michelson and German opticians. It is also due to the progress of technological processes of manufacture, particularly in the region of metallurgy. The designer has at his disposal a variety of materials of differing physical properties. He can thus depend upon obtaining the material he desires; and it can be ground to the shapes he desires within narrow limits of tolerance. These instruments have put thought on to a new level. A fresh instrument serves the same purpose as foreign travel; it shows things in unusual combinations. The gain is mere addition; it is a transformation."[15]

The half-century or so since Whitehead wrote this has seen the development of a further wealth of equipment, both conceptual and technical. The technical advances which Whitehead mentions, and other advances since his time, most notably the advent of computer age, have opened up new fields of enquiry, and new possibilities for the discovery of truths about the world, is too obvious to need elaboration here. Similarly, in the case with our conceptual apparatus, which has been enriched by concepts such as relativity, quanta, indeterminancy, and the like.

To sum up: The premise No. 2 or conjunct (2) is false because it mistakenly identifies the growth of human knowledge with the growth of scientific knowledge. Since this conjunct is false, the whole conjunction, that is, the argument itself, is false.

REFERENCES

1. Popper, K.R. *The Poverty of Historicism,* Routledge & Kegan Paul, London, 1972, p. 3.
2. Popper, K.R. *Conjectures and Refutations, The Growth of Scientific Knowledge,* Routledge & Kegan Paul, London, 1972, p. 336.
3. Popper, K.R. *The Poverty of Historicism,* Preface, v and vi.
4. *Ibid.,* Preface vi.
5. *Ibid.,* p. 140.
6. *Watkins, J.W.N.* 'Methodological Individualism: A Reply', *Philosophy of Science,* Vol. xxii, 1955.
7. Popper, K.R. *The Open Society and Its Enemies,* Routledge and Kegan Paul, London, 1966, p. 98.
8. Popper, K.R. *The Poverty of Historicism,* pp. 62–63.
9. *Ibid.,* p. 62.
10. Daniel, S.C. 'Objectivity and History: A Case Study of North East India', *Proceedings of North East India History Association,* (ed) D.R. Syiemlieh, Kamala Art Press, Shillong, 1993, pp. 33–43.

11. According to Jagat Pal, Historians explain human occurrences in terms of 'causes' and sometimes in terms of 'intentions' and 'plans' etc. He is right in saying so. However, it may be pointed out historians also explain human 'events' on the basis of trends. This they do by extrapolating the available trends. I believe that he will have no difficulty in accepting that this sort of extrapolation is a kind of reason giving explanation, which is inferential in character because of the fact that there is a movement taking us from the *explanan* to an *explanandum*. As far as human action is concerned sometimes causes are given as reasons. (Jagat Pal, "An Inquiry Concerning Historical Explanation", in *Ibid.*, p. 41).
12. Burke, T.E. *The Philosophy of Popper*, Manchester University Press, Manchester, 1983.
13. Popper, K.R. *The Poverty of Historicism*, Preface, v.
14. Professor J.B. Bhattacharjee, one of the well-known and influential historians of North-East India brings out the same point in the context of history of technology. He laments over the fact that historians of India especially of North-East India have not paid adequate attention to the history of technology. I cannot even conceive of improving upon what he says. Therefore, I would like him to speak for himself. He says: ". . ., the historical analysis based on technological development — the 'techno-historical method', if we may call it — may enable the historian to formulate a causal law for development studies to suggest that under the presence of certain antecedents, or initial conditions a particular event or development is likely to happen. He may be able to predict that when the antecedents or conditions are same, the consequence or development is also bound to be the same. Technology, including possible innovation and improvement in the object over a period of time, is likely to reach the closest proximation of a truth to be experienced in future." (J.B. Bhattacharjee, "Technology, Social Formation and Historical Inquiry" Presidential Address - History Archaeology and Culture Session, XVII *Indian Social Science Congress*, 1993, p. 16).
15. Whitehead, A.N. *Science and the Modern World*, Cambridge University Press, Cambridge, 1926, p. 143f.

Bibliography

Books

Barpujari, H.K. *Political History of Assam* (Three Volumes), Government of Assam, Dispur, Gauhati, 1970-1980.

Barpujari, H.K. *American Missionaries and North-East India (1836-1990 A.D.)*, Spectrum Publication, Gauhati, Delhi, 1986.

Bhattacharya, N.N. *Religious Cultures of North-Eastern Region*, Manohar, 1995.

Bhattacharjee, J.B. *Pre-Colonial North East India, Har Anand*, Publication in association with Vikas Publishing House Pvt. Ltd., 1991.

Bhuyan, S.K. *Some Literary Reminiscences*, Pragjyotish Grandhasala, Gauhati, Assam, 1954.

Burke, T.E. *Sciences and Modern World*, Diver Publications, New York, 1986.

Carver, Terrell (ed). *The Cambridge Companion to Marx*, Cambridge University Press, 1992.

Choudhury, J.N. *The Khasi Canvas*, Shillong, 1978.

Cohen, G.A. *Karl Marx's Theory of History: A Defence, Princeton*, N.J.: Princeton University Press, 1978.

Collingwood, R.G. *The Idea of History*, Oxford University Press, 1956.

Collingwood, R.G. *An Essay on Metaphysics*, Oxford University Press, 1940.

Croce, B. *La Storia Come Pensiero e Come Azione*, Laterza and Figli, Bari, 1938.

Descartes, Rene. *A Discourse on Method*, (Trans.) John Veitch, Everyman's Library, London, J.M. Dent and Sons Ltd., 1949.

Guha, Amalendu. *Planter Raj to Swaraj – Freedom Struggle And Electoral Politics in Assam, 1826-1947*. People's Publishing House, New Delhi, 1988.

Hegel, G.W.F. *The Philosophy of History*, Diver Publications, New York, 1956.

Hume, David. *A Treatise of Human Nature*, (ed.) L. A. Selby-Biggs, Oxford University Press, 1888.

Kamenk, G. *Marxism and Ethics*, Macmillan, St. Martin's Press, New York, 1969.

Kant, Emmanuel. *Critique of Pure Reason*, (Tr.) Norman Kemp Smith, Macmillan, 1973.

Kant, Emmanuel. *Foundation of Metaphysics of Morals*, (Tr.) L.W. Beck, Chicago, 1950.

Kant, Emmanuel. *Critique of Judgement*, (Tr.) J.C. Meredith, Oxford, 1952.

Kant, Emmanuel. *Critique of Practical Reason*, (Tr.) L.W. Beck, New York, 1956, V: 10/115.

Kant, Emmanuel. *Religion Within the Limits of Reason Alone*, (Tr.) T.M. Greene and H.H. Hudson, VI: 5/5. Lowith, Karl. *Von Hegel Zu Nietzsche.*

Marx, Karl and Engels, Frederick. *Collected Works*, New York and London, International Publishers, 1973.

Popper, K.R. *The Open Society and Its Enemies*, Routledge and Kegan Paul, London, 1966.

Popper, K.R. *Conjectures and Refutations, The Growth of Scientific Knowledge*, Routledge and Kegan Paul, London, 1972.

Popper, K.R. The Poverty of Historicism, Routledge and Kegan Paul, London, 1972.

Sangma, M. *History and Culture of the Garos*, Books Today, New Delhi, 1981.

Sri Aurobindo, *Social and Political Thought*, Vol. 15, Sri Aurobindo Ashram, Pondicherry, 1971.

Von Wright, Georg Henrik. *Explanations and Understanding*, Routledge and Kegan Paul, 1971.

Whitehead, A.N. *Science and Modern World*, Cambridge University Press, 1926.

Articles

Bhattacharjee, J.B. "Technology, Social Formation and Historical Inquiry", Presidential Address, Archaeology and Culture Session, *XVIII Indian Social Science Congress*, 1993.

Bhattacharjee, J.B. "North East Indian Perspectives of History", Presidential Address, *Proceedings of North East India History Association*, Fourteenth Session, Jorhat, 1993, Kamala Art Press, Shillong, 1994.

Daniel, S.C. "The Logic of Historical Analysis: Reflections on North-East Historiography", *Proceedings of North East India History Association*, Twelfth Session, Jagi Road, 1991, Kamala Art Press, 1991, Kamala Art Press, Shillong, 1992.

Hume, David. "Of the Study of History", *The Philosophical Works of David Hume*, (ed.) T.H. Greene and T.H. Grosse, London: Longman, Green and Co., 1898.

Jagat Pal, "An Enquiry Concerning Historical Explanation", *Proceedings of North East India Association*, Thirteenth Session, Shillong, 1992, Kamala Art Press, Shillong, 1993.

Passmore, J.A. "The Objectivity of History" in *Philosophical Analysis and History*, (ed.) William H. Dray, Harper and Row, New York and London, 1966.

Reiman, Jeffrey. "Moral Philosophy: The Critique of Capitalism and the Problem of Ideology" in *The Cambridge Companion to Marx*, Carver Terrell (ed.), Cambridge University Press, 1992.

Syiemlieh, D.R. "The Robert Lindsay Muniments", *Proceedings of North East India Association*, Twelfth Session, Jagi Road, 1991, Kamala Art Press, Shillong, 1992.

Syiemlieh, D.R. "The Beginning of the Catholic Church Among the Mizos", *Proceedings of North East India Association*, Thirteenth Session, Shillong, 1993, Kamala Art Press, Shillong, 1994.

Syiemlieh, D.R. "Thomas Jones' Injudicious Marriage?", *Proceedings of North East India Association*, Fourteenth Session, 1994, Modern Offset, Shillong, 1995.

Watkin, J.W.N. "Methodological Individualism: A Reply", Philosophy of Science, Vol. XXII, 1955.

Windelband, W. Geschichte and Naturussemchaft, Reprinted by J.C.B. Mohr, Tubingen, 1907.